RE-DISCOVERING The Making of the UK

BRITAIN 1500-1750

Colin Shephard
Tim Lomas

Series Editor:
Colin Shephard

Consultant Editor:
Terry Fiehn

JOHN MURRAY

Titles in this series:

Re-Discovering Medieval Realms – Britain 1066–1500 Pupils' Book	0 7195 8542 2
Re-Discovering Medieval Realms – Britain 1066–1500 Teachers' Resource Book	0 7195 8543 0
Re-Discovering The Making of the UK – Britain 1500–1750 Pupils' Book	0 7195 8544 9
Re-Discovering The Making of the UK – Britain 1500–1750 Teachers' Resource Book	0 7195 8545 7
Re-Discovering Britain 1750–1900 Pupils' Book	0 7195 8546 5
Re-Discovering Britain 1750–1900 Teachers' Resource Book	0 7195 8547 3
Re-Discovering The Twentieth Century World – a world study after 1900 Pupils' Book	0 7195 8548 1
Re-Discovering The Twentieth Century World – a world study after 1900 Teachers' Resource Book	0 7195 8549 X

The Schools History Project

The Project was set up in 1972, with the aim of improving the study of history for students aged 13–16. This involved a reconsideration of the ways in which history contributes to the educational needs of young people. The Project devised new objectives, new criteria for planning and developing courses, and the materials to support them. New examinations, requiring new methods of assessment, also had to be developed. These have continued to be popular. The advent of GCSE in 1987 led to the expansion of Project approaches into other syllabuses.

The Schools History Project has been based at Trinity and All Saints College, Leeds, since 1978, from where it supports teachers through a biennial Bulletin, regular INSET, an annual conference and a website (www.tasc.ac.uk/shp).

Since the National Curriculum was drawn up in 1991, the Project has continued to expand its publications, bringing its ideas to courses for Key Stage 3 as well as a range of GCSE and A level specifications.

Words printed in SMALL CAPITALS are defined in the Glossary on page 113.

Note: The wording and sentence structure of some written sources have been adapted and simplified to make them accessible to all pupils, while faithfully perserving the sense of the original.

© Colin Shephard, Tim Lomas 1995 with revisions by Terry Fiehn 2001

First published in 1995 as *Discovering The Making of the UK* by
John Murray (Publishers) Ltd,
50 Albemarle Street,
London W1S 4BD

This completely revised edition first published 2001, reprinted 2001, (twice), 2002

All rights reserved. No part of this publication may be reproduced in any material form (including photocopying or storing in any medium by electronic means and whether or not transiently or incidentally to some other use of this publication) without the written permission of the Publisher, except in accordance with the provisions of the Copyright, Designs and Patents Act 1988 or under the terms of a licence issued by the Copyright Licensing Agency.

Layouts by Alison Bond/Bondi Design
Artwork by Countryside Illustrations, Jon Davis/Linden Artists, Patricia Ludlow/Linden Artists, Janek Matysiak, Tony Randell, Steve Smith
Colour separations by Colourscript, Mildenhall, Suffolk
Typeset in 11½/13pt Concorde by Wearset, Boldon, Tyne and Wear
Printed and bound in Great Britain by Butler & Tanner, Frome and London

A catalogue entry for this title is available from the British Library

ISBN 0 7195 8544 9
Teachers' Resource Book ISBN 0 7195 8545 7

Contents

Introduction	1
How did Britain change between 1500 and 1750?	2
Your pathway	4

▶ SECTION 1

Was this a good time to be living in England?	5
England in the 1500s	6
Were the poor really poor?	10
Were the rich really rich?	16
Family life	24
Review: Was this a good time to be living in England?	30

▶ SECTION 2

Why was there so much religious change in the sixteenth century?	31
Catholic versus Protestant	32
Why did Henry VIII make himself head of the Church in England?	34
How did Henry close down the monasteries?	36
How did Edward change English churches?	40
Could Queen Mary make England Catholic again?	42
What were the secrets of Elizabeth's success?	44
Were the Catholics framed?	56
Review: Why was there so much religious change in the sixteenth century?	60

▶ SECTION 3

Why did civil war break out and did it change anything?	61
Why did civil war break out in 1642?	62
What was life like during the Civil War?	72
Why did the English execute their King?	80
Why did they want the King back?	84
The same old story?	92
Review: A different kind of monarchy	94

▶ SECTION 4

How modern was Britain in the 1700s?	95
A Scientific Revolution?	96
How did London change?	100
A tour around Britain	106
Review 1500–1750: 'A picture of the period'	112
Glossary	113
Index	114
Acknowledgements	115

 **1534** Henry VIII replaces the Pope as head of the Church in England

 **1588** England defeats the Spanish Armada

 **1605** The Gunpowder Plot

1500 **1550** **1600**

INTRODUCTION

1642–46 The English Civil War

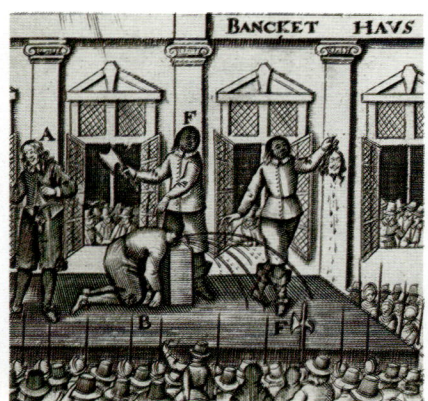

1649 Charles I is executed

1660 Charles II becomes King and the monarchy is restored

1650   **1700**   **1750**

How did Britain change between 1500 and 1750?

Changes you can see

One of these pictures shows England in 1500. The other shows England in 1750. Discuss what changes you can see. Are there a lot of changes, or not many?

Changes you can't see

Some of this book is about changes you can see. But most of it is about changes you can't see. It is about changes in *beliefs* and *attitudes*. They do not usually leave marks on the landscape but they are still very important, possibly even more important than the changes you can see.

Your pathway

In this book you will find out about changes that took place in Britain between 1500 and 1750.

Section 1: Was this a good time to be living in England?
Life was changing for rich and poor throughout the period. For example, you will find out:

- why there were so many more poor people and why the rich were worried about them

- how family life was changing.

Section 2: Why was there so much religious change in the sixteenth century?
In the 1500s England changed from Catholic to Protestant. You will investigate how and why. For example:

- Why did Henry VIII make himself head of the Church in England?

- How did Mary try to make England Catholic again?

Section 3: Why did civil war break out and did it change anything?
In the 1600s conflict between the King and Parliament over who should govern England led to the Civil War. You will explore:

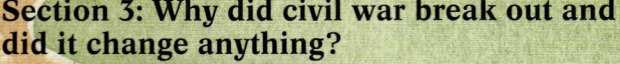

- why the King and Parliament quarrelled

- why Parliament decided to get rid of the King altogether and, why, eleven years later, they wanted the King back.

Section 4: How modern was Britain in the 1700s?
This section tells you about some other features of life in this period, for example:

- people's ideas – were they scientific or superstitious?

- London – was it a modern city?

SECTION 1

WAS THIS A GOOD TIME TO BE LIVING IN ENGLAND?

A wedding feast!
A rich gentleman has invited all his friends to celebrate: to eat, drink and dance. Everyone is having a good time.

Is this typical of England at this time? In this section you are going to decide for yourself if this was a good time to be living in England.

England in the 1500s

▶▶ If you had travelled through England in the 1500s what would you have seen? And how different was it from England today? Over the next four pages you'll find out.

- In 1500, most of the land in England had not been altered by humans. There were huge areas of forest where wild pigs, wild cats and even wolves still lived. Much of the rest of the land was wasteland, covered in scrub and thickets.
- Only a small part of the land was farmed. And an even smaller part of this was used for growing crops. Most of the farm land was used for grazing sheep. There were about eight million sheep and only about 2.7 million people! The sheep were kept to supply wool for the cloth industry.
- Nine out of ten people lived in the countryside and worked on the land. Most villagers lived on what they could grow. If they grew more than they needed they sold the surplus in the local market town. For most ordinary villagers it was often a struggle just to keep their families fed. To make a little extra money they did some spinning and weaving.
- Cloth making was England's most important industry. Nearly every town had a group of spinners, weavers and dyers.
- Most towns were little more than overgrown villages. The townspeople kept cattle on common land in the town and every week the streets were filled with the noise of cattle coming to market.

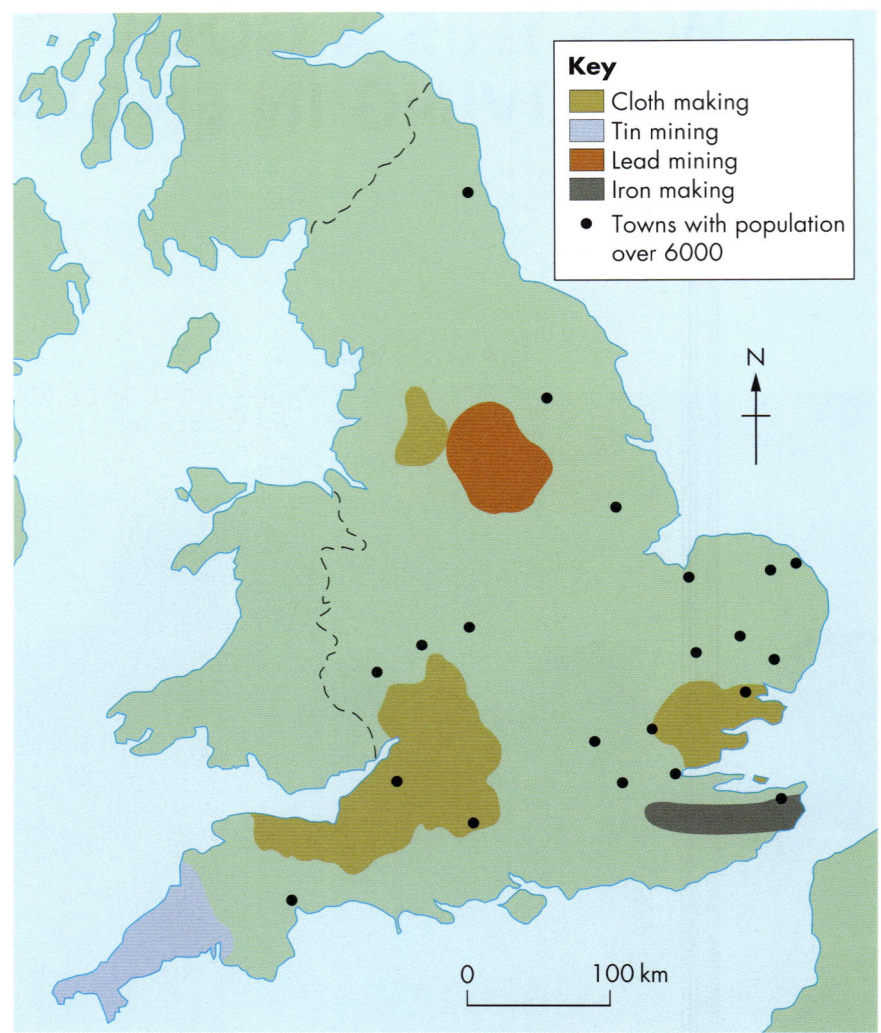

▲ **SOURCE 1** *England in 1500*

▼ ACTIVITY

From the information on this page make a list of differences between England in the 1500s and England today. Use the following headings for your list:

- population
- towns
- jobs
- the countryside.

Social groups

One sixteenth-century writer said, 'We in England divide our people into four groups: gentlemen, citizens, yeomen and labourers.' What life was like depended a great deal on which of these groups you belonged to.

ENGLAND IN THE 1500s

▼ SOURCE 2

▲ SOURCE 3

▲ SOURCE 4

▲ SOURCE 5

▼ SOURCE 6

▼ ACTIVITY

Here are five pictures showing life in the 1500s. You can use these pictures to work out what life was like.

1. Draw a table like the one below.

Source	What is happening in the picture?	What social group does it show?	What evidence is there that it shows this social group?

2. Working in pairs, look at Sources 2–6. Think about what you can see in each picture. What is happening? For example, are people working, playing, getting food or fighting? Write a detailed description in column two of your table.
3. Look back at the social groups on page 7.
   a) Think about which social group each of Sources 2–6 shows. Remember: the source doesn't tell you this – you will need to work it out, or INFER it, from the evidence in the picture. Write your answer in column three.
   b) Think about what evidence in each source supports your choice of social group. Write your answer in column four.
4. Which of the following statements do you most agree with? Explain your choice by referring to Sources 2–6.

   - Life in this period was unpleasant and hard.
   - Life in this period was comfortable and pleasant.
   - Life in this period was hard for some people but pleasant for others.

Were the poor really poor?

▶▶ In the sixteenth and seventeenth centuries one of the most serious worries for the government was the problem of poor people.

The big question was: did they really need help? Rich people could not decide whether the poor should be given money and food, or be whipped and made to work! In this enquiry you are going to try to understand why rich people were so confused about the poor.

Reasons to be suspicious!

The drawings in Source 1 show beggars or VAGRANTS who could be seen on the streets of England in the sixteenth century. All but one were described in a popular book by Thomas Harman. He claimed that beggars were not really as helpless as they made out. He said that they deliberately avoided working, preferring to make their living by begging, robbing and stealing because it was easier!

▼ ACTIVITY

1. Study Source 1.
   a) Match captions A–H to pictures 1–8.
   b) What evidence is there that not all the people on this page are poor and helpless?
   c) Why do you think so many people used tricks to beg?
   d) Which two tricksters should people be most worried about?
   e) Write a paragraph to explain why rich people were suspicious of beggars. You could start:

   Rich people were suspicious of beggars because...

   For example...

▼ EXTRA

2. Picture 6 shows Nicholas Jennings, a famous vagrant. Your teacher will give you more information about him.
   Design a 'Wanted' poster, showing what he looked like and why he was dangerous.

▼ SOURCE 1

A A **Rogue** will crawl along the streets (supporting his body by a staff) as if there were not strength in his legs. His clothes are all tattered.
Rogues are not driven to this poverty. If they had better clothes they would rather sell them, to move people to pity.

B The **Upright Man** is the king of vagrants. He carries a staff. He doesn't beg, but demands that people give him money. He helps himself to other vagrants' possessions and even to their women.

C The **Counterfeit Crank** pretends to be ill. He sucks soap to make himself foam at the mouth and then he pretends to have an epileptic fit.

D The **Doxy** carries on her back a great pack in which she has all the things she has stolen. As she walks she knits, and wears a needle in her hat. If any chickens are near she feeds them with bread, and has a thread tied to a baited hook. The chicken swallows this, is choked and is then hidden under her cloak.

G **Bawdy Baskets** are women and go with baskets on their arms. In these baskets they have laces, pins and silk of all colours. They will steal linen clothes off hedges. They get from maidservants, when their mistress is out of the way, some good piece of beef, bacon or cheese, that shall be worth 12d, for 2d of their toys.

E **Clapper Dudgeons** lay crowfoot and salt upon the place of the body they wish to make sore. They then put on it a linen cloth till it stick fast. When plucked off it leaves raw flesh. They cast over that a bloody filthy cloth. With their women they travel from market to market. They are able by begging to get five shillings in a week. They often have six or seven pounds on them.

H **John Burr**, 54 years old, is a glazier. He is very sick and cannot work. Alice, his wife, spins. They have seven children, the eldest is 20 years of age and the youngest two years. They can spin wool. They have always lived here.

F The **Abraham Man** walks with a sheet around his body. He is often bare-armed and bare-legged. He pretends to be mad by whooping and bellowing and staring with a wild look.

WERE THE POOR REALLY POOR?

Reasons to be sympathetic!

Now you are going to look at the other side of the story. There may have been some fakes – beggars who used tricks to get people to give them money – but there were also many genuine poor people. You should have found one of them in amongst the tricksters on the previous two pages.

In some ways the genuine poor were better off than vagrants. They did at least have somewhere to live and a few belongings. Source 2 shows a typical home. As long as harvests were good they managed to feed their children and look after the old and sick in their families. But when harvests were bad, or they got sick or old and there was no one to look after them, they had to beg or they would starve to death.

▼ **SOURCE 2** *A reconstruction of the inside of a cottage in the 1500s. This shows Thomas Herries with all his belongings. These were recorded in an* INVENTORY *when he died in 1599. There would have been other poor people who owned a lot less than Thomas Herries or who lived in much tattier houses. Some houses would have had earth floors*

PROBLEMS IN THE 1500s

Column 1: developments

Monasteries closed down
During hard times monasteries gave poor people food and shelter. But Henry VIII closed them all down.

Bad harvests
There were a lot of bad harvests during the sixteenth century. Sometimes farmers lost most of their crops.

Rising population

Sheep farming
Landowners changed to sheep farming because they earned more money from breeding sheep for wool than from growing crops for food.

Fencing off common land
Landowners fenced off common land which the poor used to use. Instead they used the land for grazing sheep.

Higher rents

Column 2: effects

Looking after sheep required fewer people than growing crops, so people lost their jobs.

The poor had nowhere to grow their own vegetables or rear animals and were forced to buy expensive food.

After a bad harvest there was not enough food to go around and prices rose. Poorer people could not even afford to eat bread because the price of wheat had increased so much. In 1597, after three years of bad harvests, there was widespread famine in England.

Labourers were made homeless if they could not pay their rents.

There wasn't enough food or jobs for the rapidly increasing number of people. Many left their villages to search for work and other ways to survive.

People had no one to help them if they were sick, ran short of food or were made temporarily homeless.

▼ ACTIVITY

Column 1 describes the developments which affected the poor in the 1500s. Column 2 explains how each development affected poor people.

1. Decide which effect fits with which development.
2. Combine them and write out six complete cause cards using your own words to explain the causes of poverty.
3. When thinking about causes it can help to put them into categories. Classify your cause cards into two groups:
   a) those caused by people
   b) those caused by events beyond the control of people.
4. Now change the categories, and sort them into the following:
   a) causes to do with farming
   b) causes that have nothing to do with farming.
5. Choose two causes which you think made life particularly hard for poor people living in the country.
6. Write a paragraph to explain the reasons for being sympathetic to poor people in the 1500s. Use the examples you selected for Question 5 to support your main point. You could begin:

There were many reasons for being sympathetic to poor people in the 1500s. For example...

WERE THE POOR REALLY POOR?

What did rich people do about the poor?

On pages 10–11 you saw the reasons why rich people were suspicious of the poor. On pages 12–13 you saw the reasons why they were sympathetic. It was all very confusing for people at the time. They did not know what to do.

Response one: 'Flog 'em and hang 'em'

To start with the government passed harsh laws to deal with the problem of beggars and vagrants.

> **1531**
> If a healthy man or woman is a vagrant and cannot give a full explanation of how he lawfully earns a living, he shall be stripped naked, tied to the end of a cart and whipped through the town until his body is bloody. He shall then return to the place where he was born.

> **1547**
> Anyone unemployed for three days is to be termed a vagrant, and shall be branded with a 'V' and given as a slave for two years to the person who reported him as a vagrant.
> In return for bread and water he must do everything his master tells him. If he refuses he should be whipped or imprisoned with iron rings around his neck and legs. If a slave runs away twice he can be executed.

Response two: 'Help some, be hard on others'

When these laws did not solve the problem the government decided there were two different problems which needed two different solutions. So it classified the poor into two groups:

- the **deserving poor** – people who were poor as a result of some personal disaster
- the **idle poor** – people who deliberately avoided work and tried to live off others.

In 1601, the government passed a new Poor Law. It lasted for 200 years. It was a great success.

> ▼ **SOURCE 3** *From the 1601 Poor Law*
>
> The churchwardens of every PARISH shall...
>
> - raise weekly by taxation of richer people... money to provide wool, thread and iron to set the poor to work
> - pay money towards the relief of any lame, old, blind or other people who are not able to work
> - make the children of some poor learn a trade
> - send to jail or to a house of correction any who refuse to work
> - whip until bloody any vagabond and send him back to his home.

▲ SOURCE 4

> ▼ ACTIVITY
>
> 1 Look at Source 4 which shows a scene around 1550. Use the information on page 14 to work out what offence the men at A and B may have committed.
> 2 Why do you think these punishments were so harsh?
> 3 Look at Source 3. How had the treatment of the poor changed since 1547?
> 4 Why do you think attitudes to the poor were changing?
> 5 Some rich people were against the new Poor Law. Can you work out why?
> 6 Write a paragraph to explain how the 1601 Poor Law was different from earlier laws. You could begin:
>
>   *The new Poor Law was different from earlier laws because...*
>
>   *For example...*
>
>   *I think this was better/worse than the old laws because...*
>
> ▼ DISCUSS
>
> 7 'We would never treat homeless people today like they did in the sixteenth century.' Do you agree?

Were the rich really rich?

▶▶ You are probably better off than poor people in the 1500s. But how do you compare with the rich? You are going to decide by examining the homes and belongings of some rich families and comparing them with your own.

The houses of the rich

▼ **ACTIVITY**

1. Sources 3–6 show pictures of rooms as they might have looked during the sixteenth and seventeenth centuries. Match the following labels to the correct rooms:
   - bedroom
   - kitchen
   - long gallery
   - dining room.

2. Choose either the bedroom or the kitchen. Compare it with the kitchen or a bedroom in your home. What are the similarities? What are the differences? Which one would you rather live in, and why?

3. All the rooms in Sources 3–6 are found in the houses shown in Sources 1 and 2. See if you can match them up. Explain your choices.

4. Think about your own home.
   a) Make a list of the main items of furniture and equipment.
   b) Underline five items that your family could not do without. Compare your list with a list made by someone else in the class.
   c) Which of the items that you can't live without did they have in the sixteenth and seventeenth centuries? Try to find them in Sources 3–6.

▲ **SOURCE 1** *The Old House, Hereford*

▲ **SOURCE 2** *Hardwick Hall, Derbyshire*

▲ SOURCE 3

▲ SOURCE 5

▲ SOURCE 4

▼ **DISCUSS**
Based on what you have seen on these two pages, do you think you have a better, or a worse, standard of living than rich people in the sixteenth and seventeenth centuries?

▲ SOURCE 6

WERE THE RICH REALLY RICH?

How did the homes of the rich change?

For many rich people the sixteenth and seventeenth centuries were a time of peace and prosperity. Lots of new houses were built. Some of these new houses were now built of stone or brick instead of wood.

Furnishing

Inside, many of the rooms had wooden panels on the walls instead of the tapestries which had been used in medieval times. Floors were usually made of wood, though cobbles or stones were still used in the servants' areas. Ceilings in the main living rooms were plastered, often with delicate patterns (see inset). Fireplaces became more usual, even in smaller rooms. Kitchens often had large fireplaces. Dogs were sometimes bred to run inside a wheel that turned a spit in front of the fire. Hot ashes were put in the wheel to make the dogs run faster.

Privacy

People's living habits were changing. They wanted more privacy, so they no longer lived together in a large hall. There were separate rooms for resting, sleeping and eating. The rich slept in four-poster beds, although generally people had a lot less furniture than we do today. Houses were built with corridors so servants or guests did not come wandering through at any moment. Separate staircases and corridors were built for servants. Bedrooms were upstairs and the living rooms downstairs.

Hygiene

There were few bathrooms. Baths were often taken in the bedroom. Most people used a toilet that was nothing more than a wooden seat over a bucket. The contents were thrown onto the land around the house or into nearby streams. Spitting was common. Nobody was allowed to leave the table while a meal was in progress. Some people would urinate in their boots because they could not leave the table!

Eating

The main meal in the sixteenth century was usually about midday, but by the seventeenth century breakfast at around 9a.m. and supper at 10p.m. were more popular.

▼ ACTIVITY

1. There is a lot of information packed into the text on this page. Read the text carefully and make a list of all the ways in which houses, and life inside them, had changed for the rich since the Middle Ages. You can get a sheet from your teacher to help you.
2. Which change do you think would have had the greatest impact on the way people lived? Explain your choice.

▼ EXTRA

3. Design an advertisement for the wheel-turned spit described in the text. Show what you think it looked like, explain how it worked and explain its advantages.

WERE THE RICH REALLY RICH?

What were the homes of the middle classes like?

Throughout the sixteenth and seventeenth centuries towns were growing. The number of middle-class people, traders, craftsmen, doctors and lawyers was also increasing. They were not as rich as the people on pages 16–19, but they had done well in business and had more money than they needed for the basic necessities of life.

A tradeswoman's house

> ### ▼ ACTIVITY A
> What can we learn about Mary Meighan's home from the inventory in Source 7?
> a) How many rooms were there in the house?
> b) What was each room used for? Look at the equipment and furniture in each room to help you decide.
> c) What trade do you think Mary Meighan carried out? Give three reasons for your answer.

▼ **SOURCE 7** *An extract from the inventory of the house of Mary Meighan of Shrewsbury. She died in 1660*

In the kitchen
2 small tables
1 cupboard
1 bench
2 chairs
4 small stools and all the panelling
1 large screen on glass
3 shelves to hold books

In the parlour
2 tables
1 cupboard
2 benches
3 joint stools
2 small carpets
1 cupboard cloth
8 cushions and all the panelling
1 chair
Pewter
Iron ware

In the chamber over the parlour
1 small table
1 bench
1 chest
1 standing bedstead
1 truckle bed [a small bed on wheels]
1 twin chair
1 feather bed
1 flock bed
2 bolsters
2 blankets
2 pillows
1 covering, curtains and valance for 1 bed
1 panelled door

In the chamber over the kitchen
2 standing beds
1 wardrobe
2 chests
3 coffers
Panelling
Bedding, curtains, valance, linen ware

In the room on the stair head
1 little cupboard and 1 truckle bed
1 basin
1 door with panelling
Bedding
Clothing

In the tanhouse
82 tanned hides
6 horse hides
Dozen calf skins
4 loads of bark
1 lead pump
1 bark mill
3 gutters
2 tubs
All other tanning implements
1 cow and 1 hog
Charcoal

In the servants' chamber
1 flock bed and clothes
4 silver spoons
Hemp and flax

A merchant's house

Sources 8–10 are pictures of a house built at the end of the sixteenth century by a Plymouth merchant. Plymouth was a busy port and one of the most important towns in England at this time. The house is still standing today.

▲ SOURCE 8

◄ SOURCE 9

▼ SOURCE 10

▼ ACTIVITY B

1 Draw up an inventory, in the style of Source 7, for the contents of the two rooms in Sources 9 and 10.
2 You are an 'estate agent' in the sixteenth century. It is your job to advertise either Mary Meighan's or the merchant's house for sale. Design a leaflet. (It might help you to look at estate agents' adverts in your local newspaper. But remember, people in the sixteenth century would expect a different kind of house from people today.)

WERE THE RICH REALLY RICH?

What was it used for?

▼ ACTIVITY

1 Objects from the sixteenth and seventeenth centuries can tell us a lot about the way people lived at the time.

Of course it is best to look at real objects that you can touch and smell and look inside. But if you aren't lucky enough to have access to a cupboard full of sixteenth- and seventeenth-century objects you can use photos.

You can see a number of objects that belonged to people in the sixteenth and seventeenth centuries in Source 11. You are going to try to work out from the photos:

- what each object was used for
- whether it was owned by a rich person, a person from the middle classes or a poor person.

As you look at each object write a detailed description of its shape, size, colour, texture and the materials it is made from. Fill in your own copy of the table below as you work your way through the objects. Don't worry if you feel unsure of your answers.

Object	Description	What is it used for?	Who might have owned it?

▼ EXTRA

2 Over the past twelve pages you have looked at the lives of the rich and the poor. If people from the sixteenth century had to leave five things in a time capsule to show people in the twenty-first century what their lives were like, what would be the five best things for:
a) a rich person
b) a person from the middle classes
c) a poor person
to leave?

15cm

50cm

80cm

▲ **SOURCE 11** *Objects from the sixteenth and seventeenth centuries*

4

30cm

7

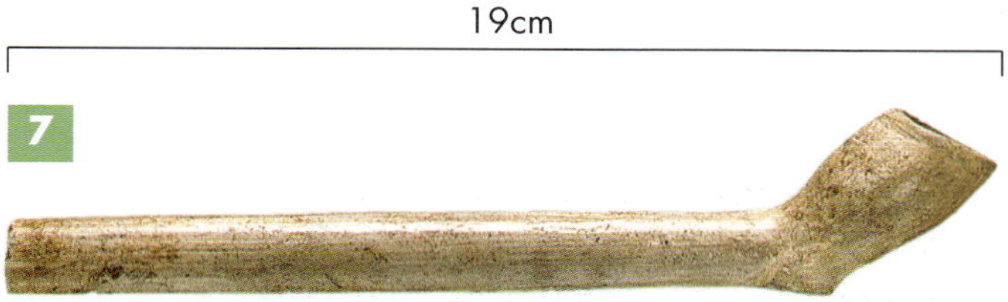

19cm

5

11cm

8

60cm

6

20cm

9

28cm

10

40cm

Family life

▶▶ **Much of this book is about kings, queens and governments. But the private lives of people and their families are just as important. What was family life like in this period? You are going to use a range of sources to make up your own seventeenth- or eighteenth-century 'magazine' about family life.**

Two family portraits

Nowadays almost everyone has a camera. But cameras were not invented until the nineteenth century. Before then, if you wanted a record of your family you asked an artist to paint a family portrait. This was very expensive so only rich people could afford it. There are no portraits of poor families from this period.

▼ ACTIVITY

Today there are lots of magazines for parents. You are going to work in groups to design one for parents in the seventeenth or eighteenth century. Each of you will research and write a different piece for the magazine and then put them together using ICT. Here are some ideas for things you could include in your magazine:

- a 'Family of the month' feature, based on a recent portrait of an interesting family
- 'How to survive childbirth', an article on the perils of childcare and recent advances made in childbirth
- 'Ten top tips for taming tiny tots' – ten pieces of advice for modern-minded eighteenth-century parents about how to bring up children
- 'Are you happily married?', a questionnaire to find out if people are happy in their marriages.

Over the next six pages, stars like this will give you ideas you can use for your articles. Your teacher can give you a planning sheet to help you as well.

And, as you work through the enquiry, discuss the questions on the sources as you go.

Idea
For your magazine you could give advice on what makes a good family portrait.

▼ DISCUSS

Examine Sources 1 and 2.

1. How many children did each family have (think carefully)?
2. Do you think the children are wearing their everyday clothes or their best clothes?
3. Which family do you think is richest?
4. Why do you think the family in Source 1 asked the artist to paint the baby's rattle and the bird on the table?
5. Why do you think the family in Source 2 asked the artist to paint the skulls in the background?
6. What evidence do these pictures give that many children died young?
7. Which family would you rather belong to? Explain your choice.

▶ **SOURCE 1**
Lord Cobham and his family, painted in 1567. His wife is sitting beside him. His elder sister, who is probably unmarried, is on the right

▶ **SOURCE 2**
A family portrait painted in 1645. The skulls in the background represent the children who died as infants

FAMILY LIFE

Married life

Historians know a good deal more about married life in this period than they did about marriage in the Middle Ages. It became fashionable for rich people to keep diaries and write letters or autobiographies, and a lot of these have survived. However, they only tell us about the rich (most poor people could not read or write so did not keep diaries) and they usually tell us more about men's attitudes than women's.

▼ **SOURCE 3** *Some of the things that historians have found out about marriages in this period*

- Men believed that they were best at making decisions and making money.
- Women were expected to be maternal, domestic and obedient. The wife's main job was to produce male heirs.
- Some marriages were very loving, but husbands and wives usually spent little time together.
- Marriages were short. One of the partners usually died before the children were very old, so couples did not grow old together. Many men married again after their wives died in childbirth.
- Divorce was very uncommon.
- Wife sales took place among ordinary people. They were a kind of divorce. Both husband and wife could agree to it and the wife would accept a new husband.
- Married women had few rights. Husbands were masters over their wives. As soon as they got married, everything a woman owned became her husband's.
- A husband had the right to beat his wife if she was troublesome (as long as the stick was no thicker than a man's thumb) or even use a scold's bridle like this if she nagged too much.
- At the beginning of the sixteenth century rich parents arranged their children's marriages. By 1750 children had a greater say and sometimes married for love.
- Children of poorer people were much freer to choose their husbands and wives.
- Rich people often married in their late teens. Poor people often married later, when they were in their late twenties.

It is important to remember that people are individuals. Every relationship is different. It is hard to generalise about marriages. Sources 4 and 5 give snapshots of two contrasting marriages.

▼ **SOURCE 4** *Extracts from the diary of Samuel Pepys*

2 May 1663 I slept till almost 7 o'clock. So up and to my office (having had some angry words with my wife about her neglecting to keep the house clean, I calling her a 'beggar' and she calling me a 'prick-louse'). Returned home to dinner. Very merry and well pleased with my wife.

19 December 1664 I was very angry and began to find fault with my wife for not commanding the servants as she ought. She gave me an angry answer. I did strike her over her left eye such a blow, as the poor wretch did cry out. But her spirit was such that she scratched and bit me.

12 July 1667 ... And so home, and there finding my wife in a bad mood for my not dining at home, I did give her a pull by the nose. I decided to go back to the office to avoid further anger. She followed me in a devilish manner, so I got her into the garden out of hearing (to avoid shame) and managed to calm her. Then I walked with her in the garden, and so to supper, pretty good friends, and so to bed.

▼ **DISCUSS**

Examine Sources 4 and 5.

1. Which of the following words would you use to describe Samuel Pepys' marriage:
   - boring
   - peaceful
   - stormy
   - loving
   - exciting.

   Give reasons for your answer.
2. How is Lucy Hutchinson's marriage different from the Pepys'?
3. Who was more equal with her husband: Elizabeth Pepys or Lucy Hutchinson?
4. Pepys' diary was written for himself. Lucy's account was written for her children about their father. Which account do you think is more reliable for telling us what the marriage was really like?
5. A lot of evidence about people's private lives in the seventeenth and eighteenth centuries comes from diaries and autobiographies. Why should we be careful about believing everything someone says in a diary or an autobiography?

▼ **SOURCE 5** *Lucy Hutchinson wrote this for her children after her husband died. In the style of the time she calls herself 'she'*

He managed the reins of government with love and she delighted in his government. He governed by persuasion. So generous was he to her that he would never receive an account of what she had spent. So constant was he in his love that when she ceased to be young and lovely he began to show most fondness.

Idea
For your magazine you could include a letter from a husband or a wife about their relationship.

FAMILY LIFE

Childbirth and childcare

Women were kept busy in the home having children and looking after them. Since there was little in the way of birth control, many women were pregnant for most of their child-bearing years. Although women had lots of babies, many did not survive. Childbirth was also dangerous for the mother.

In the sixteenth century

In the sixteenth century about one in five babies died before their first birthday. There were many reasons for this: clumsy delivery of the baby at birth, neglect and the dirt and squalor many babies were brought up in.

Parents in the sixteenth century tried not to get emotionally involved with their children because they expected them to die. It was common to give a newborn child the same first name as one that had just died. The new baby was seen as a replacement.

▼ **SOURCE 6** *Information taken from the autobiography of Sir Simonds D'Ewes about his childhood. D'Ewes came from a rich family*

December 1602 A bungled delivery damaged his right eye at birth. He could never use it for reading.

5 months old He was sent to a wet nurse for several months.

1–8 years old He was sent to his grandfather's house. His grandparents were not there so he was brought up by servants. His parents only visited him twice.

8 years old He was sent to a boarding school.

Idea
For your magazine you could include a 'My story' feature in which Sir Simonds D'Ewes writes about his childhood.

▼ **DISCUSS**

1. Look carefully at Source 7. It shows a mother who has just given birth. Find three dangers in the room that might put the newborn baby's life at risk.
2. Read pages 28–29 and list five bad things about the way children were treated in the sixteenth century.
3. Draw up another list of five improvements that were made by 1750.

◀ **SOURCE 7** *A sixteenth-century engraving*

Most rich mothers sent their babies to WET NURSES until they were about eighteen months old. The death rates for these babies was twice as high as for babies who stayed with their mothers.

Babies were often bound in swaddling clothes for at least the first four months of their lives. They could not move their heads or limbs. This was supposed to make their limbs grow straight, but it also meant the babies did not need constant attention. They could be left, hanging on pegs, wallowing in their own excrement for hours. Many parents would not even let older children crawl about because they thought crawling was animal-like behaviour.

Children as young as three or four were dressed as little adults. Daughters in rich families were encased in corsets reinforced with iron. This was intended to make sure they walked gracefully, but their lungs were sometimes damaged. Parents aimed to turn children into adults as quickly as possible. Beatings were common and many children grew up fearing their parents.

Improvements by 1750

By 1750, the death rate for babies was falling. Fewer babies died during birth. Better designed forceps, rather than the hooked instruments, were used.

Childcare was generally improving. It became more common for mothers to breastfeed their babies. Wet nursing was criticised. Swaddling was used less too. Parents wanted to cuddle their children, which you cannot do if they are swaddled. Parents grieved when young babies died. Children were seen as different from adults.

▼ **SOURCE 9** *Thomas Coram's reasons for setting up the London Foundling Hospital in 1741. In the first four years 15,000 children were brought to the hospital*

To prevent the frequent murders of poor miserable children at their birth and to take in children abandoned in churchyards or in the streets.

Idea
For your magazine you could include an appeal for funds by Thomas Coram.

▼ **SOURCE 8** *From a book on childcare, written by Dr Cadogan in the 1700s, criticising how wet nurses looked after babies*

When [the baby] cries, he is hung from a nail like a bundle of old clothes and while the nurse attends to her business the child remains thus crucified. All who have been found in this situation had a purple face because the blood could not circulate. The baby was believed to be content because he did not have the strength to cry out.

A wet nurse, drawn in 1664

Idea
For your magazine you could draw up a notice, using Source 8, warning parents against using wet nurses.

Review: Was this a good time to be living in England?

▼ REVIEW ACTIVITY A

1. In 100 years' time historians may want to study you and your life, just as you have studied the lives of people in the sixteenth, seventeenth and eighteenth centuries. List at least ten types of source which they would find useful for finding out about you. For example, how could they work out what you eat, what you do in your spare time, what you wear and what your home is like?
2. Write a paragraph about your sources, explaining to a historian of the future why these sources will be useful and making them aware of any sources they should be careful about using.
3. Make a list of the different types of historical sources you have studied on pages 6–29. The artwork above will jog your memory.
4. Discuss the similarities and differences between these historical sources and the sources a historian of the future would use to find out about you.

▼ REVIEW ACTIVITY B

5. You are going to consider whether the period 1500–1750 was a good time to be living in England. Draw up at least three statements about life in this period which can be supported by sources from pages 6–29.
6. Use your statements to create a class display.

SECTION 2

WHY WAS THERE SO MUCH RELIGIOUS CHANGE IN THE SIXTEENTH CENTURY?

1548 They are clearing everything out of Melford church.

1555 They are putting everything back in again.

1562 They're clearing it out once more.

Welcome to Melford! Are you confused? If so, you are not alone. In the sixteenth and seventeenth centuries religion was very important, but also very confusing. In this section you will find out why. By the end you should be able to explain quite well what is going on in Melford.

Catholic versus Protestant

▶▶ For over a thousand years England had been a Catholic country. Then in the 1500s things began to change. There was a choice! There was the Catholic way and the Protestant way. Over the next two pages you are going to find out how they are different.

The Catholic way

In 1500 virtually every person in England was a Catholic. These are some of the Catholic beliefs.

The altar is the focal point of the church. It should look spectacular. There should be ornaments and candlesticks on it.

Churches should be highly decorated with paintings and coloured windows showing God's glory and power and mystery.

People need priests to help them find God. The priest acts as a link between an individual and God.

Priests should wear special clothes to reflect their special status as the link between God and man. They should not get married, but should devote their lives totally to God.

The Pope is head of the Church. God appointed him. He best knows what God wants the Church to do. The way to salvation is to follow the teachings of the Church.

What you believe about God and the way you practise your religion is very, very important. If you do not worship in the right way you will go to hell for eternity.

The Pope and his bishops can forgive sins. People can show they are sorry for their sins if they give a gift to the Church.

The Bible and church services should be in Latin as they have been for one thousand years.

> ▼ **ACTIVITY**
>
> Compare Catholic beliefs with Protestant beliefs.
> 1. What do Catholics and Protestants:
>   a) disagree about?
>   b) agree about?
> 2. a) Write down two things which a Protestant might say is wrong with Catholic beliefs.
>   b) Write down two things which a Catholic might say is wrong with Protestant beliefs.

The Protestant way

In the early 1500s, a growing number of people felt deeply that the Catholic Church had lost its way.

- They said the Catholic Church was **too rich**. People gave the Church lots of money, but the bishops and monks spent it on fine clothes and palaces instead of on helping the poor.
- They said that Catholic priests and monks were **corrupt and lazy** and did not do their jobs properly. They said that some priests never even visited their parishes, leaving someone else to take their services.
- They said it was wrong that Catholic services and the Bible were still in **Latin**. Protestants said it was hard to feel close to God if you do not understand the services or read the Bible yourself.
- They were particularly angry that the Catholic Church allowed rich people to **pay a bishop or the Pope to have their sins forgiven**. They said that only God could forgive sins.

Because they were protesting about the Catholic Church, these people were called Protestants. The movement for reform that they started is called the Reformation. One of the most important reformers was a German called Martin Luther, whose ideas soon spread to other countries including England.

These are some of the Protestant beliefs.

Churches should be simple and plain. A simple church brings people closer to God. The altar should be replaced by a wooden table and there should not be any ornaments, which distract people from focusing on God.

Ministers should wear simple robes. They are ordinary people. They should be free to marry like ordinary people.

Jesus Christ is head of the Church. Christ is more important than a human leader, like the Pope. The way to salvation is to follow the teachings of Jesus Christ. Only Jesus can forgive sins.

People do not need priests to help them find God. Believing in Jesus Christ is the way to find salvation.

The Bible and services should be in English so people can understand them.

What you believe about God and the way you practise your religion is very, very important. If you do not worship in the right way you will go to hell for eternity.

Why did Henry VIII make himself head of the Church in England?

▶▶ **When Henry VIII first heard about Luther's Protestant ideas he wrote a book defending the Catholic faith. The Pope thought that Henry was such a good Catholic that he gave him the title 'Defender of the Faith'. Twenty years later, however, Henry VIII did a massive U-turn. He replaced the Pope as head of the Church in England. You are going to find out why and how he did this.**

Henry was bankrupt. He wanted to be powerful in Europe. He had already fought some very expensive wars in Europe and desperately needed more money to continue his campaigns. His personal life was also very expensive. Yet the Church had lots of money. If only he could get hold of some of it.

I need money

Henry's problems

I want a son

Henry's wife, Catherine of Aragon, had given him a daughter, Mary, but no son. Catherine had had several miscarriages and it was clear that the chances of her giving birth to a healthy son were small. Henry believed that to make sure the Tudor dynasty survived he had to have a son. But to have a son he needed a new wife. And to get a new wife he needed a divorce. Only the Pope, the head of the Church, could give him a divorce.

I want power

Henry wanted to control the Church. Since medieval times there had been struggles over whether priests should obey the Pope or the King. (You will remember the battle between Archbishop Becket and King Henry II that led to Becket's murder.) The powerful monasteries were loyal to the Pope. Henry VIII resented this. He wanted to control the Church in his own country.

If I control the Church in England then...

▼ ACTIVITY A

Look carefully at Henry's problems. Then complete Henry's sentence to show how becoming head of the Church in England might help him solve his problems.

ACTIVITY B

1. Look at Henry's solutions below. Complete the following sentences to explain, in your own words, how making himself head of the Church in England solved Henry's problems.
   a) It solved Henry's need for an heir because …
   b) It solved Henry's need for money because …
   c) It gave Henry more power because …
2. Which of the statements in the opposite column do you most agree with? Explain your answer and support it with evidence from these two pages.

- Henry could not decide whether he supported the Catholics or the Protestants.
- Henry did not really care about religion. He supported whoever would help him get what he wanted.
- Henry was a Catholic at heart. He only supported Protestant ideas because they could help him get what he wanted.
- Henry was a Protestant at heart. He only followed Catholic ways because he was used to them.

Henry's solutions

He made himself head of the Church

He said that the Pope no longer had any authority in England. From now all priests and monks had to do what Henry said, not what the Pope said.

He gave himself a divorce

He divorced Catherine of Aragon and married the pregnant Anne Boleyn, hoping for a son.

He bullied any opposition

Once Henry had control of the Church, he persecuted those who opposed him. He even cut off the head of his close friend, Thomas More, because More would not accept Henry as head of the Church.

He took over the monasteries

From 1536–39 he closed all the monasteries, taking all their gold and silver ornaments and all their land. This brought him an enormous amount of money. Many of the monasteries fell into ruins or were turned into private houses.

He sat on the fence!

These measures might make Henry sound like a Protestant. Think again. Henry made himself head of the Church in England, but that did not make him a Protestant! In fact, he passed a law saying the Church still had to hold Catholic services, and he didn't change the inside of churches at all.

How did Henry close down the monasteries?

▶▶ As you saw from the previous spread there is no doubt as to why Henry wanted to close down the monasteries – he wanted their wealth. However even an all-powerful Tudor king could not simply have said, 'I'm closing the monasteries down because I want their money'. He had to have some evidence to justify his actions. How did he get this evidence?

It is sunrise. The monks are waking up and getting ready to begin their daily chores. The rider was up before them. He has ridden all night to get here. This is the tenth monastery he's visited in a week. He can't stop here for long. He has just a few hours to dig up as much scandal about this place as he can. He spurs his horse on, down the slope towards the monastery. What will he find?

▼ **SOURCE 1** *Monastic rules*

Monks and nuns were meant to live according to strict rules laid down by St Benedict in AD500. These rules made sure they devoted their lives to God and to helping other people. The rules said they should:

- live as poor people
- not marry or have sex
- look after the poor, the sick and the old
- give food and shelter to travellers
- eat simply and wear simple, rough clothes
- copy out precious manuscripts.

In 1535 Thomas Cromwell, Henry's Chief Minister, sent out hand-picked inspectors to report on the state of the monasteries. He was looking for excuses to close them down. The inspectors were given clear instructions.

Please report to me on:

- the names of monks who are breaking monastic rules (see Source 1). I am particularly interested in the sex lives of monks and nuns
- the names of any discontented monks or nuns who want to leave their monasteries
- any 'superstitious' practices, particularly if they involve holy relics. [Relics were items that had once belonged to, or been touched by, a saint. Monasteries made a lot of money from people who came on pilgrimage to see or touch relics]
- each monastery's income and its debts.

The inspectors did not visit all the monasteries they reported on. Instead of a personal visit they often just asked people living close by to tell them what the monastery was like. Reports which praised the monasteries were sent back to the inspectors with instructions from Cromwell to be more critical. There are extracts from the reports on the next page.

HOW DID HENRY CLOSE DOWN THE MONASTERIES?

▼ **SOURCE 2** *Extracts from some of the reports Cromwell received*

a) *About Crossed Friars monastery, London*

Found the prior at that time in bed with a woman, both naked, about 11 o'clock in the morning.

b) *About the monastery in Bath*

I have visited Bath, and found the prior a very virtuous man, but his monks more corrupt than any others in vices with both sexes. The house is well prepared but £400 in debt. I am sending to you some of their relics – Mary Magdalene's comb and St Dorothy's and St Margaret's combs. They cannot say how they got them.

c) *About Langdon in Kent*

I spent a good time knocking at the abbot's door, neither sound nor sign of life appearing. I found a short pole-axe standing behind the door, and with it I dashed the door to pieces. About the house I go, and find his woman.

d) *About Woolsthorpe in Lincolnshire*

The abbot is well beloved, having eight religious persons, being priests of right good conversation and living religiously, having such qualities of virtue as we have not found the like in any place.

e) *About St Edmund's monastery, in Suffolk*

The Abbot delighted much in playing at dice and in that spent much money. For his own pleasure he has had lots of beautiful buildings built.

f) *About St Edmund's convent*

I could not find out anything bad about the convent, no matter how hard I tried. I believe I couldn't find anything because everybody had got together and agreed to keep the convent's secrets . . . Among the relics we found were the coals that St Lawrence was burnt upon, the clippings of St Edmund's nails, St Thomas of Canterbury's penknife and his boots, and enough pieces of the Holy Cross to make a whole cross.

g) *About the monastery at Battle*

The Abbot is 'the veriest hayne, beetle and buserde, and the arentest chorle that ever I see.' The House is 'so beggary a house I never see, nor so filthy stuff . . . the stuff is like the persons.'

▼ **ACTIVITY**

1 Look at Source 2.
   a) What evidence is there of monks or nuns breaking monastic rules?
   b) Which of the reports would Cromwell have been pleased with? Which would he have sent back for a more critical rewrite?
2 Extracts a)–f) have been simplified for you so that they are easier to understand, g) has not. Discuss what you think it means with a partner. Then try to rewrite it in modern English like the others.
3 In your study of history you will come across many biased sources. The reports in Source 2 are some of the most obvious and extreme examples. If you wanted to find out what monastic life was like at this time you would have to be very suspicious about these reports.
   a) Write a list of all the reasons why they should be mistrusted.
   b) Explain whether these reports can still be useful to a historian. Think carefully before you answer.

The end of the monasteries

The reports gave Henry what he needed. The Act to destroy the monasteries began: 'Since great sin and abominable living is daily committed...the possessions of such houses should be converted to better uses and the unthrifty religious persons in them be forced to reform their lives...'

Henry's commissioners met almost no resistance. At Hexham in Northumberland the monks barred the gate and prepared to resist the commissioners by force. At Norton in Cheshire the abbot trapped the commissioners inside and then raised a small army and laid siege to his own monastery! But these were notable exceptions. Almost everywhere things went without a hitch. The monks accepted the inevitable. The local people hardly protested at all. And the rich fell over themselves to buy the valuable monastery land from Henry.

By 1539 not one functioning monastery was left in England. Henry's normal income was about £500,000 a year. Between 1536 and 1547 he received an extra £140,000 a year from the dissolution of the monasteries.

If our inspector had returned twenty years later, this is what he would have found!

How did Edward change English churches?

▶▶ **Although Henry got rid of the Pope and closed the monasteries, he didn't do much else to make England a Protestant country. But, after he died, his son Edward made massive changes.**

Henry VIII died in 1547. His son, Edward VI, was only nine years old. And, as you'd expect, his advisers told him what to do, think and say. They were Protestant and they encouraged him to make many changes to religion. In just six years the buildings, decorations and services in thousands of churches across England changed completely.

The changes pleased the Protestant minority but they upset the majority of English people.

People in many areas tried to ignore the changes. They had enjoyed saints' days and Church Ales (festivals) as holidays from their busy working lives. They did not like new beliefs and practices being forced upon them. And, although you can change the inside of a church or a prayer book very quickly, you cannot change people's beliefs quite so easily. Many people genuinely believed that the Protestant way was wrong. They worried that if they changed the way they worshipped they would end up in hell. The battle between Catholics and Protestants was far from over.

▶ **SOURCE 1** *Inside a typical Roman Catholic Church in 1500*

▼ **SOURCE 2** *Changes to the Church of England in Edward's reign*

- A new Prayer Book was introduced. Services were now said in English, not Latin.
- The Catholic MASS was abolished and replaced with the Protestant Holy Communion service. According to this service the bread and wine represented the body and blood of Jesus Christ, but did not actually become the body and blood of Christ as it does during Mass. Holy Communion was a service of remembrance, not a sacrifice.
- Churches were changed.
- Priests were told to dress in simple clothes, not fine robes. They could now get married.
- Many old traditions were swept away: saints' days were abolished, decorating the church with holly and ivy at Christmas was banned and Church Ales were stopped.
- Some beliefs were changed. For example, you could no longer buy your way into heaven.

▼ **ACTIVITY**

1 Copy this table.

	A Catholic church has:	A Protestant church has:
Changes you can see	Stained glass windows	Plain glass windows
Changes you cannot see		

2 Use Sources 1 and 3 to complete the first row of your table. You can get a copy of the sources from your teacher to help you if you wish.

3 Use Source 2 to complete the second row. You may also need to refer back to pages 32 and 33.

4 Write down three things that you think a Catholic would have said about the changes made to the Church during Edward's reign.

5 Look back at the picture on pages 32–33. Draw or describe who was winning the tug of war:
a) when Henry VIII was King
b) when Edward VI was King.

◀ **SOURCE 3** *Inside a typical church during Edward's reign*

Could Queen Mary make England Catholic again?

▶▶ Edward VI died in 1553. His sister Mary became Queen. She was a devout Catholic who believed that no one in England would be able to go to Heaven unless the Roman Catholic Church was brought back. Could Mary make England Catholic again? She thought so. See if you agree.

Can she do it?

Mary has called her advisers together. Could she make England Catholic again?

> There are powerful Protestants in England. They hate the Pope and Catholicism.

> Your father, Henry VIII, closed all the monasteries and sold their land to rich and important people. You would have to reclaim all this land.

> England has only been Protestant for six years. Before that, England was Catholic for centuries.

> Most English people still prefer the old Catholic ways to the new Protestant ways.

> With respect, your Majesty, you are 37, unmarried and have no children. Your sister Elizabeth, who will be Queen after you, is a Protestant.

> Four hundred of the most important Protestant leaders have fled to Europe.

> When Edward died Protestants tried to replace you, but they received no support.

▼ ACTIVITY A

1. a) Copy the table on the right.
   b) Look at the statements made by Mary and her advisers. Decide which column of the chart they should go in and give reasons for your choice.
2. Looking at all the factors together, on a scale of 1–5 (1 = no chance and 5 = very good chance), how good do you think Mary's chances were of making England Catholic again?

Factors which suggest that Mary had a good chance of making England Catholic again	Factors which suggest that Mary did not stand much chance of making England Catholic again

How did she try to do it?

In 1554 Mary married King Philip II of Spain. Spain was the most powerful Catholic country in Europe.

Between 1555 and 1558 Mary had 284 Protestants burned to death. She was hoping that this would persuade other Protestants to return to Catholicism.

She brought back the old Catholic Prayer Book and services in Latin. Altars were brought back, decorated windows re-installed, and priests were given back their fine robes.

▼ **ACTIVITY B**

Study Sources 1 and 2. What evidence can you find that the author/artist was a Protestant?

▼ **SOURCE 2** The execution of Latimer and Ridley

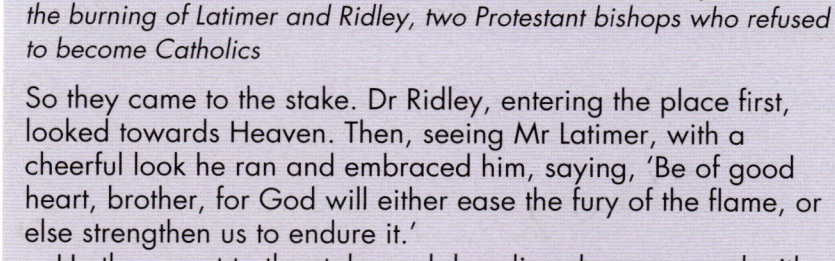

▼ **SOURCE 1** An extract from John Foxe's Book of Martyrs, about the burning of Latimer and Ridley, two Protestant bishops who refused to become Catholics

So they came to the stake. Dr Ridley, entering the place first, looked towards Heaven. Then, seeing Mr Latimer, with a cheerful look he ran and embraced him, saying, 'Be of good heart, brother, for God will either ease the fury of the flame, or else strengthen us to endure it.'

He then went to the stake and, kneeling down, prayed with great fervour, while Mr Latimer following, kneeled down and prayed also. Dr Ridley gave presents of small things to men standing near, many of whom were weeping strongly. Happy was he who could get the smallest rag to remember this good man by. Then the blacksmith took a chain of iron and placed it about both their waists and then knocked in the staple.

Dr Ridley's brother brought him a bag of gunpowder and tied it about his neck. His brother did the same to Mr Latimer.

They then brought a lighted faggot and laid it at Dr Ridley's feet. Upon which Mr Latimer said, 'Be of good comfort, Mr Ridley, we shall this day light such a candle, by God's grace, in England, as I trust never shall be put out.'

Mr Latimer cried out, 'Father of Heaven, receive my soul', and soon died with seeming little pain. But Dr Ridley, due to the bad arrangement of the fire (the faggots being green and piled so high, that the flames were kept down by the green wood), laboured in much pain until one of the bystanders pulled the faggots with a hook. Where Ridley saw the fire flame up, he leaned himself to that side. As soon as the fire touched the gunpowder he was seen to stir no more. The dreadful sight filled almost every eye with tears.

Maybe Mary would have succeeded. Maybe not. We will never know, because she died in 1558 at the age of 42. And, just as her advisers predicted, her Protestant half-sister became Queen.

What were the secrets of Elizabeth's success?

▶▶ **Elizabeth became Queen in 1558 and reigned for 45 years. After the crises of the previous twenty years, her reign is sometimes called a golden age and Elizabeth is seen as a strong, successful queen. How did she do it? This is what you will explore as you read Elizabeth's tips for success. At the end, you will use what you have found out to write Elizabeth's OBITUARY.**

Tips for success: tip one

Don't get married!

Elizabeth was a young woman in a man's world. She had not expected to be Queen. Her sister Mary had died suddenly, leaving her to rule a country torn by religious divisions. Everyone expected Elizabeth to marry soon after she became Queen, so that she had a husband to make the decisions for her while she got on with producing a male heir. That's what queens were expected to do. But Elizabeth never married. It was not for want of willing husbands – she received plenty of proposals from foreign princes and there were plenty of English nobles who would have liked to marry her. She even had affairs with some of her admirers. But she never became a wife. Some say that this was the secret of her success.

Options

I could marry Philip of Spain, as my sister did. This would give us a powerful ally and make England a power to be reckoned with in Europe. But...

I could marry a nobleman from a powerful English family. But...

I could marry a foreign prince – Charles of Austria wants to marry me. It would help to have a connection with a foreign country. But...

I could marry Robert Dudley. He is good looking, I enjoy his company and his wife has just died. But...

▼ ACTIVITY A

1. a) Look at Elizabeth's thoughts about her possible husbands.
   b) Match each option with the disadvantages choosing that husband would bring. Be careful, you might want to match two or three disadvantages with some husbands.

   You will find this task easier if you put the options and disadvantages on cards. You can get some cards from your teacher.

Disadvantages

> ...if I keep them guessing, they will all want to marry me and that will keep them loyal and trying to get my favour.

> ...I don't want to marry the same man as my sister.

> ...a husband might try to control me and take over the running of the country. Many people already think that a woman is too weak to be a strong ruler on her own.

> ...the English do not like foreign rulers, especially Catholic ones. There was a rebellion after Mary married Philip.

> ...I can't make up my mind. There are just too many handsome men.

> ...what if he wanted to use England to help fight his country's wars with other countries. We don't want to get mixed up in other people's squabbles.

> ...if I marry one of them, the others will be jealous of his power. They might start a rebellion.

▼ ACTIVITY B

2. As you work through the information and tasks on pages 44–45, make notes that you can use for writing Elizabeth's obituary.

   Note down two ways in which not getting married helped Elizabeth stay strong and be successful.

> **Elizabeth's tips for success: note one**
>
> By not getting married she . . .
>
> (Clue: the problems of a strong or foreign husband)
>
> (Clue: the advantages of keeping everyone guessing)

Tip one-and-a-half: be careful who you choose as your advisers

Elizabeth didn't rely on a husband for advice, instead she used advisers. Some historians believe that one of the reasons Elizabeth was successful was that she had excellent advisers. For example, William Cecil, Lord Burghley, helped her make important decisions and worked behind the scenes to ensure that powerful nobles supported her.

Other historians argue that this is a sexist comment made by male historians. If they find a successful woman in history they automatically assume that there must be a clever man guiding her.

Nevertheless, there is little doubt that Elizabeth was either good at choosing her advisers or very lucky.

WHAT WERE THE SECRETS OF ELIZABETH'S SUCCESS?

Tip two

Compromise over religion... but be tough with extremists.

When Elizabeth became Queen, England was bitterly divided over religion. Religious war was a real possibility. Protestant and Catholic EXTREMISTS both posed a threat to Elizabeth.

THE PROBLEM

Protestant extremists

By 1558 more than half the people in England were Protestant. Some of them were extremists called Puritans. They wanted Elizabeth to wipe out all traces of the country's Catholic past. Some even wanted her to persecute Catholics in the same way that Mary had persecuted Protestants. Their aim was to get rid of Catholicism in England once and for all.

Catholic extremists

There were still many Catholics in England. Their beliefs had not changed just because they had a new queen. They saw the Mass as the only way to true salvation. The Pope sent priests to England to hold secret Masses and to try to keep Catholicism alive in England. These priests were often given special hiding places in the homes of rich Catholics. Many people thought they spied for Catholic countries. Catholic extremists wanted to get rid of Elizabeth and place a Catholic monarch on the throne.

Elizabeth

Elizabeth was a moderate Protestant. She realised that there could not be two competing religions in the same country. She also wanted to heal the divisions and hatred of the past. She wanted greater tolerance. Elizabeth wanted a Church everybody could belong to.

▼ ACTIVITY

1. Note down two ways in which the method Elizabeth used to handle religious problems made her seem successful.

▼ EXTRA

2. Look again at the picture on pages 32–33, and what you wrote for Question 5 on page 41. Now draw or describe who was winning the tug of war:
   a) when Mary was Queen
   b) when Elizabeth was Queen.

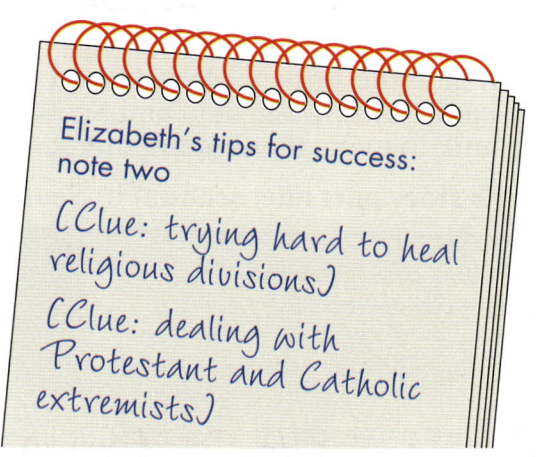

Elizabeth's tips for success: note two

(Clue: trying hard to heal religious divisions)

(Clue: dealing with Protestant and Catholic extremists)

ELIZABETH'S SOLUTION

What she did about Protestant extremists

Elizabeth showed the Protestant extremists that she was not going to be pushed around. When a book was written that she did not agree with, she had the author's hand cut off.

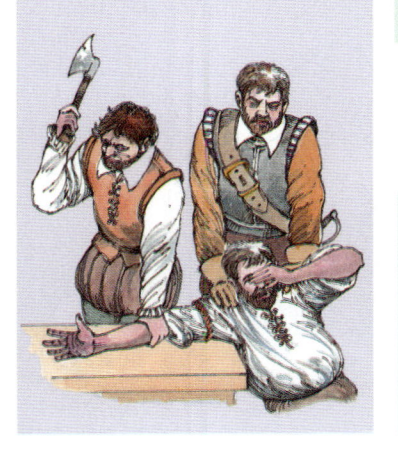

What she did about the Church

Elizabeth took a 'middle road'. She made Protestantism the official religion in England. She brought back the changes made in Edward's reign – including the new Prayer Book, the Bible in English and simpler churches – and priests were again allowed to marry. However, she refused to give way to extreme Protestant ideas. She did not persecute ordinary Catholics, but she did fine them for not attending church. She kept some aspects of the old Catholic Church. For example, she kept bishops and cathedrals, allowed churches to continue using crosses and candles, and let the priests wear special VESTMENTS.

What she did about Catholic extremists

Elizabeth sent the same message to the Catholic extremists as she did to Protestant extremists. When a Catholic priest, Edmund Campion, tried to convert people to Catholicism he was arrested, tortured and hanged. When some Catholics plotted to replace her she dealt ruthlessly with the rebellion.

The result

Her policy of tolerance worked. More and more people moved towards her type of Protestant Church, and her tough treatment of extremists prevented ideas spreading.

WHAT WERE THE SECRETS OF ELIZABETH'S SUCCESS?

The life and death of Mary, Queen of Scots

Let's step aside from Elizabeth's tips for success for one moment and look at the story of Mary, Queen of Scots. Mary was Elizabeth's cousin. England and Scotland were rivals at this time and, to make the situation more tense, Mary was Catholic.

Mary's story part one: scandal in Scotland

1 Mary's early life was full of scandal... She was widowed at 20.

2 Her second husband, Darnley, was a drunk who was so jealous that he murdered her private secretary.

3 Darnley was strangled one year later and Mary made off with the main murder suspect, the Earl of Bothwell.

4 A group of Protestant Scottish nobles were fed up with Mary's behaviour. They put her in prison, but she escaped to England in 1568.

Mary's story part two: prison and plots in England

5 Once in England Mary became Elizabeth's problem. Mary wanted to be Queen of England and she was a Catholic. Parliament feared that Mary would become a focus for every Catholic plotter who wanted to get rid of Elizabeth.

> Mary, Queen of Scots, is bent on destroying Her Majesty Elizabeth. Mary is a fierce, hard and desperate woman. As long as she lives Her Majesty will not be safe. Mary is poisoned with Catholicism and is burning with a desire to destroy Protestantism in England.

6 Mary denied involvement in any Catholic plots. But, to be on the safe side, Elizabeth kept her under guard in castles around England for eighteen years.

7 Year after year Elizabeth's adviser, Walsingham, claimed to have uncovered Catholic plots against Elizabeth. Leading plotters were executed.

8 Walsingham was sure that Mary was involved in these plots, but he didn't have any proof. Then, in 1586, he got hold of a coded message written by Mary to a Catholic, called Anthony Babington, who was planning to kill Elizabeth. Some historians say that Walsingham forged this evidence. However, it was enough to persuade Elizabeth that she should remove the threat against her once and for all.

9 Mary was executed in 1587, at Fotheringay Castle.

▼ ACTIVITY

Write down two ways in which Elizabeth's treatment of Mary, Queen of Scots, helped her to be successful.

WHAT WERE THE SECRETS OF ELIZABETH'S SUCCESS?

Tip three

Win a great victory over a foreign power

Elizabeth has refused to marry me.

She has helped Spain's enemies in the Netherlands.

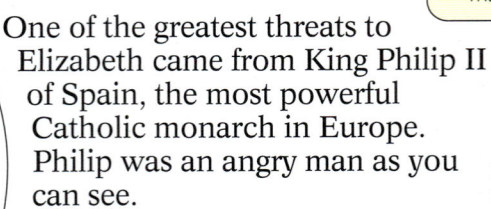

She is making England a Protestant country.

One of the greatest threats to Elizabeth came from King Philip II of Spain, the most powerful Catholic monarch in Europe. Philip was an angry man as you can see.

Philip decided to teach Elizabeth, and England, a lesson. In 1588 he sent a great Armada – a fleet of ships – to invade England. If things went according to plan, the Armada would smash the English navy and help a great Spanish army land in England. They would be helped by English Catholics to get rid of Elizabeth. But things did not work out as he had hoped.

She has executed Mary, Queen of Scots – a Catholic queen!

And, to add insult to injury, English sea captains are attacking my ships and stealing my treasure.

1 The English navy attacked the Spanish fleet while it was in disarray. Many Spanish ships were damaged and around 1000 Spaniards were killed. No English ships were sunk and only about 50 sailors killed.

2 The Spanish fleet tried to sail back to Spain but was hit by terrible storms. About 44 ships were wrecked and thousands of Spanish sailors drowned. There was joy and relief all over England at the news of the Armada's defeat.

3 Elizabeth makes a speech at the time of the Armada.

I am resolved in the midst of heat and battle to live and die amongst you all. I know that I have the body of a weak and feeble woman, but I have the heart and stomach of a King, and of a King of England too.

England had been threatened by a great invasion force and had triumphed. It is always good for a leader's reputation to win a victory over a foreign enemy. Elizabeth had appeared as a brave and courageous leader throughout. The Queen immediately had a special portrait of herself painted so that people would connect her with this great victory for ever.

▼ **SOURCE 1** *The 'Armada portrait', painted in 1588*

Elizabeth is standing in a strong pose in what looks like the cabin of a warship. It suggests she was present as the Armada headed towards the English coast, and as it was defeated.

Elizabeth's hand is on a globe to show she is Empress of the world.

The pearls around Elizabeth's neck and on her dress show how wealthy England is.

▼ **ACTIVITY**

Write down two ways in which the defeat of the Armada helped Elizabeth to be seen as a strong queen.

Elizabeth's tips for success: note three

(Clue: what would have happened if the Armada had succeeded?)

(Clue: the way people saw Elizabeth after its defeat)

WHAT WERE THE SECRETS OF ELIZABETH'S SUCCESS?

Tip four

Maintain an image

You will remember that when Elizabeth came to the throne, many people doubted that a woman could govern a country by herself. Elizabeth had to show her people that she could be a strong ruler.

One of the best ways to boost her image and win loyalty was to tour the country and let people see her. She could demonstrate how rich and powerful she was. These tours were successful, but she could only visit a limited number of places. So, she also used portraits to spread her image around.

Elizabeth wanted to impress her subjects. You have just seen how she had a portrait painted to show how powerful she was after the defeat of the Armada (see page 51), and how this encouraged people to see her as a strong queen. But she also had to make sure that there were no paintings around which made her look ugly, weak or old.

Elizabeth kept a tight control over the paintings of her that were available. At intervals throughout her reign, portraits of the Queen were issued which were to be copied by artists. No other portraits of the Queen were allowed. This plan seems to have worked because artists were still copying these 'official' paintings years later.

On these pages you can see some portraits and drawings of Elizabeth that were done both during and after her reign.

▲ SOURCE 2

▲ SOURCE 3

◄ SOURCE 4

▲ SOURCE 5

▶ SOURCE 6

◀ SOURCE 7

▼ ACTIVITY

1. Look at Sources 2–7. Match them with Captions A–F.
   - **A** *Painted when she was twelve years old and no one expected her to become Queen*
   - **B** *Painted at the end of her reign when she was in her sixties*
   - **C** *Painted shortly after Elizabeth's death, when people were quite relieved she had died and were glad that a new monarch was on the throne. It shows her looking old and weary.*
   - **D** *Painted twenty years after her death, when many people were looking back to the 'Golden Age of Elizabeth'. Elizabeth is seen as St George killing Catholicism represented as a dragon.*
   - **E** *Painted at the beginning of her reign when she was about 25 years old.*
   - **F** *A miniature of Elizabeth. This would have been worn around the neck in a locket, or in a ring.*

2. Which of Sources 2–7 do you think is the most reliable if you want to know what Elizabeth really looked like?

3. Look at the painting of her at the beginning of her reign and the painting of her at the end of her reign. Why do you think it is difficult to tell which is which?

4. Compare Sources 5 and 7. Did the way in which people viewed Elizabeth's reign change after her death?

5. Look at Sources 2–7 and the Armada Portrait (Source 1 on page 51). Choose the picture you think Elizabeth would have most liked to become her 'official' portrait. Explain your choice.

6. Write down two ways in which Elizabeth encouraged people to think of her as a successful queen.

Elizabeth's tips for success: note four

(Clue: visits)

(Clue: portraits)

WHAT WERE THE SECRETS OF ELIZABETH'S SUCCESS?

▼ DISCUSS

1 Look at the qualities below. Choose four that you think a good leader should have and explain why.

toughness   softness   weakness   strength   gentleness   roughness   wisdom   stupidity

tolerance   intolerance   giving in to demands   being prepared to listen to other people

being prepared to make deals   having no concern for the feelings or views of others

being hard on those who oppose you   sticking to your views even if they are unpopular

being able to make decisions

2 How far did Elizabeth have the four qualities you have chosen? Give examples from pages 44–52 to support your answer.
3 Record your ideas about Elizabeth's personal leadership qualities.

Elizabeth's tips for success: note five

Write an obituary for Elizabeth

When someone famous dies, newspapers often print an obituary, which contains a summary of their life. It is usually full of praise – no one wants to criticise someone who has just died. It is not a balanced form of writing. It is deliberately biased. Source 8 is an example of an obituary from the time.

▼ ACTIVITY

4 You are now going to use all the information you have collected about Elizabeth to write her obituary. You can use the writing frame opposite.

You could try to write in the style of the time (like Source 8) or you can write in a modern style – it does not matter. What does matter is that you get to the bottom of the story, that you understand what Elizabeth's secrets of success were. Finally, don't forget to give your obituary a headline.

▼ **SOURCE 8** *Written by Molino, an Italian visitor to England, in 1607, shortly after Elizabeth's death*

Elizabeth was the most remarkable princess that has appeared in this world for these many centuries. In all her actions she displayed the greatest carefulness which is evident from the fact that she reigned for 42 years and kept her kingdom in peace, though at the start it was full of bad feeling. But she knew how to adapt to circumstances so well that she overcame every difficulty. With her firmness she not only withstood her enemies but overpowered them.

She was beloved by her subjects, who still miss her; she was dreaded by her enemies; and in a word possessed, in the highest degree, all the qualities which are required in a great prince.

An obituary for Elizabeth

Introduction
Elizabeth was Queen of England from 1558–1603. During that time England was a strong country and she was a successful queen.

Paragraph one
Many people thought Elizabeth would not last long without a powerful husband but they were proved wrong. In fact...

Explain how not getting married helped Elizabeth. You can use what you wrote for Elizabeth's tips for success: note one to help you.

Paragraph two
One of her greatest challenges was to hold England together despite the religious divisions amongst her people. Elizabeth did this by...

Explain how she handled problems to do with religion. You can use what you wrote for Elizabeth's tips for success: note two.

Paragraph three
Elizabeth dealt with opposition from inside the country effectively. She...

Explain how she dealt with plotters. You can use what you wrote for the Activity on page 49.

Paragraph four
A successful ruler needs to keep her country safe. Elizabeth...

Explain how the Armada worked in her favour. You can use what you wrote for Elizabeth's tips for success: note three.

Paragraph five
Throughout her reign Elizabeth saw the importance of maintaining an image. She...

Explain how she promoted her image through portraits. You can use what you wrote for Elizabeth's tips for success: note four.

Paragraph six
In all her dealings Elizabeth showed qualities of leadership. For example...

Use what you wrote for Elizabeth's tips for success: note five.

Conclusion
If we look for one single thing that made Elizabeth successful it must be...

This is your overall judgement. Was her main secret of success her:
- religious tolerance
- strength of character
- refusal to let a man control her

...or something else?

Were the Catholics framed?

▶▶ Throughout this section the issue of religion has been rumbling away like a volcano. By now you might be feeling fed up with religion. Many people at the time probably were too. But the story isn't over. Far from it. In fact one of the famous episodes in the ongoing rivalry between Catholics and Protestants is yet to come: the Gunpowder Plot.

Source 1 is from a book written for children in 1835. It tells you what children at that time were taught about the Gunpowder Plot of 1605. Most people today still believe this story. But you are going to decide for yourself how accurate it is as you prepare your case for a mock trial.

▼ **SOURCE 2** *Written by an Italian visitor in 1605*

Some hold it as certain that there has been foul play and that some of the government secretly spun a web to entangle these poor gentlemen.

King James I dealt severely with the Catholics, whom he put in prison and from whom he took a lot of money. The Catholics grew tired of this. Some of them thought that if they could kill him they might have a Catholic king or queen.

From thinking wickedly they went on to do wickedly. They found that there were some cellars under the Houses of Parliament, and they filled these cellars with gunpowder; and as they expected the Parliament and the King to meet there on 5 November they hired a man called Guy Fawkes to set fire to the gunpowder, and so to blow it up and kill everybody there.

Now, it happened that one of the lords, whose name was Mounteagle, had a friend among the Catholics, and that friend wrote him a letter, without signing his name, to beg him not to go to the Parliament that day because a sudden blow would be struck which would destroy them all. Lord Mounteagle took this letter to the King's council. Some of the councillors laughed at it. But the King thought about it and said the sudden blow must mean gunpowder. He set people to watch the vaults under the Parliament, till at last they caught Guy Fawkes with his lantern, waiting for the time to set fire to the gunpowder.

◀ **SOURCE 1** From *Little Arthur's History of England* by Lady Callcott, 1835

▼ **ACTIVITY**

Some people do not accept the version of events in Source 1. They believe that the plotters were framed so that the King had an excuse to persecute the Catholics. This is not a new idea, as you can see from Source 2.

You are now going to look at some of the evidence and decide which of the following statements you most agree with.

- A It was a genuine Catholic plot.
- B The plotters were framed by Robert Cecil.

1 Make a copy of the table below.

Source	Evidence to support statement A	Evidence to support statement B

2 Sources 2–9 give you information about the plot. Study each source in turn. The questions in a star beside each source will help you understand it.
3 As you study each source record in your table any evidence it gives you to support either statement A or statement B. Remember, you will need to think hard about this. You are looking for what the source tells you about the plot, but you are also thinking about how trustworthy you think the source is. Note, you will not be able to fill in every cell in your table.
4 Finally, use your completed table to help you prepare a speech for either the prosecution or the defence at the plotters' trial.

▲ **SOURCE 3** *The Gunpowder Plotters – an engraving made soon after the plot by a Dutch artist who probably never saw them*

Choose one word which best sums up the impression Source 3 gives of the plotters.

▼ **SOURCE 4** *The Venetian Ambassador had a conversation with Robert Cecil. Robert Cecil was the King's chief minister. He was a Protestant. The Venetian Ambassador was a Catholic. According to the Ambassador this is what Cecil said:*

The King's excessive kindness has ended in this, that Catholic priests go openly about the country saying Mass. This gives great offence to others. We cannot hope for good government while we have a large number of people who obey foreign rulers as the Catholics do. The priests preach that Catholics must even kill the King to help their religion.

What does Source 4 suggest about Cecil?

▼ **SOURCE 5** *An extract from a letter sent to Lord Mounteagle. The letter was delivered to him by a disguised messenger at his London house on 26 October. This was the only night in 1605 that Lord Mounteagle stayed in his London house. Mounteagle immediately showed this letter to the King*

My lord, I have a care for your safety. Therefore I would advise you to devise some excuse to miss your attendance at this Parliament. For God and man have come together to punish the wickedness of this time. Go into the country, for they shall receive a terrible blow this Parliament – and yet they shall not see who hurts them.

1 Why do you think the messenger was in disguise?

2 Do you think the letter was intended to protect Mounteagle or to incriminate the plotters?

WERE THE CATHOLICS FRAMED?

▼ **SOURCE 6** *From Guy Fawkes' confession*

He said he did not intend to set fire to the fuse until the King came into the Houses of Parliament, and then he intended to do it so that the powder might blow up a quarter of an hour later.

A

B

▲ **SOURCE 8**
A *Guy Fawkes' normal signature*
B *His signature to his confession after he had been tortured*

★ **1** Can you suggest reasons why Guy Fawkes' signature to his confession is so different from his normal signature?
2 Does this mean that Guy Fawkes' confession cannot be trusted?

★ **1** Which of the men pictured in Source 3 does Winter's confession incriminate?
2 Can you trust the confession?

▼ **SOURCE 7** *An extract from Thomas Winter's confession. We do not know whether the confession is genuine. Cecil never showed the original confession to the court – he had a new copy written out for the trial*

We were working under a little entry to the Parliament house. We under-propped it with wood. We bought the gunpowder and hid it in Mr Percy's house. We worked another two weeks against the stone wall, which was very hard to get through. At that time we called in Kit Wright.

About Easter we rented the cellar. After this Mr Fawkes laid into the cellar 1000 sticks and 500 faggots.

▼ **SOURCE 9** *Some important facts to consider*

- At the time all gunpowder was controlled by the government. All supplies were kept in the Tower of London.
- The 36 barrels of gunpowder were placed in the cellar of a house next to Parliament. The cellar ran under the Houses of Parliament. This cellar was rented to the plotters by John Whynniard, a king's official and a friend of Cecil.
- Lord Mounteagle told the King about the plot on 27 October, yet the government took no action until 4 November.
- The government seemed to know where all the plotters were. On 7 November they were surrounded in Holbeach House. They did not resist arrest but some of them were shot dead.
- All the plotters were killed or captured quickly, except for one, Francis Tresham. He was left free until 12 December. Once the trial of the other plotters was over he was taken prisoner and died of a mysterious illness in the Tower of London on 23 December. The rumour was that he was working for Cecil all along, and that he had sent the anonymous letter to Mounteagle.

★ What do each of the points in Source 9 suggest about who might have planned the plot?

After the trial

Cecil must have been very pleased with the way events turned out after the plot. The Catholics became very unpopular. Harsher laws were passed against them. For example, Catholics could not become doctors, lawyers or government officials.

James wanted the Gunpowder Plot to be remembered. He asked people to light their autumn bonfires on 5 November. People put models of the Pope on their fires.

As for the 'plotters', they met a grisly death, as you can see from Source 10.

> ### ▼ DISCUSS
> 1 Source 10 shows the punishment of the convicted plotters. Why do you think they were punished so savagely and so publicly?
>
> ### ▼ ACTIVITY
> 2 Look again at the picture on pages 32–33. Draw or describe the situation after the Gunpowder Plot. Keep a note of your answer because you'll need it in the next section.

▼ **SOURCE 10** *A print from the time showing the execution of the plotters. After their trial for treason they were hanged, drawn and quartered*

Review: Why was there so much religious change in the sixteenth century?

▼ **REVIEW ACTIVITY**

You are now going to look back over the sixteenth century to review the religious changes that took place. This is important if you are to understand the political changes that happened in the next century. Do you remember the cartoons on page 31 about the church in Melford? You should now be able to give a good explanation of what was going on in Melford and also in England as a whole.

Use the cartoons to explain the changes in religion that took place during the reigns of Edward VI, Mary I and Elizabeth I. For each monarch, mention:
a) what changes were made
b) how Catholics and Protestants felt about the changes
c) what happened to Catholic and Protestant extremists.

1548 Edward's reign

1555 Mary's reign

1562 Elizabeth's reign

SECTION 3

WHY DID CIVIL WAR BREAK OUT AND DID IT CHANGE ANYTHING?

Many executions have taken place in English history, but this one is different from all others. The head on the block belongs to a king. After years of conflict and a bloody civil war Parliament is beheading the King of England.

Some thought that England would now be a better place. Others thought that the world was being turned upside down. See what you think, as you examine:

■ how England slipped into civil war
■ what kind of country emerged from it.

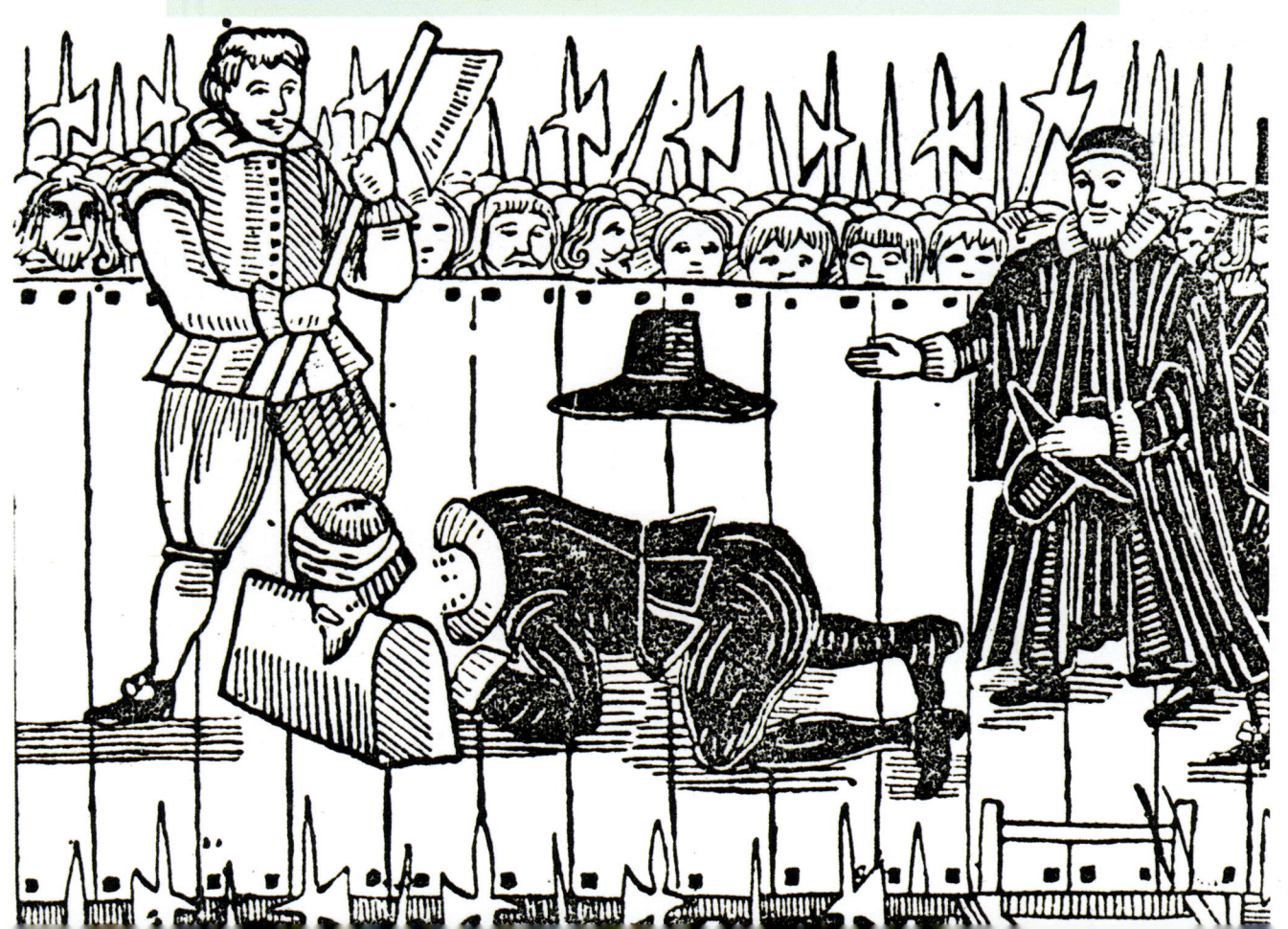

Why did civil war break out in 1642?

▶▶ On 22 August 1642 King Charles I declared war on his enemies in Parliament. During the Civil War which followed one man in ten was killed. Many people died of starvation. Others had their houses, their land or all their possessions destroyed.

How had a situation come about in which Englishmen were prepared to fight against each other, and even against members of their own families?

In this enquiry you are going to find out how England slipped into civil war.

Overview

The timeline on these pages shows you some of the important events which led to the Civil War. But it is rather misleading, because when events are laid out like this it makes the war look inevitable.

This is not how people saw events at the time. The majority of people in England – even those most closely involved in the events that led to it – had no idea a civil war was on its way until it had started.

1625

1629

Stage one: Charles gets off to a bad start

- Charles marries a Catholic.
- Parliament refuses to give Charles money, so he collects it anyway and sends Parliament home.

Stage two: Charles rules without Parliament

- Charles introduces unpopular taxes.
- Charles tries to make the Church more Cathol
- Charles tries to extend his policies to Scotland.

The background: King and Parliament
During the sixteenth century the power of Parliament had gradually been growing. By the 1620s the King of England could no longer rule the country by himself.

If the King needed money for emergencies, such as war, he had to ask Parliament to agree a tax which people all around the country would have to pay. When the King asked Parliament for a tax it had a chance to demand that he took some notice of its ideas.

▼ ACTIVITY

The Civil War was a war between the King and Parliament. One way to understand why it happened is to chart how the bad feeling built up between the two sides.

1. Draw a table like the one below to record the things each side did to annoy or antagonise the other.
2. As you work through pages 64–71 fill in your table. Start by recording items from these two pages. An example has been done for you.

Things the King did which annoyed Parliament	Things Parliament did which annoyed the King
Charles sent Parliament home and ruled without it for eleven years.	

1640

1642

Stage three: the triggers
- Parliament demands more power.
- Charles tries to arrest five MPs.
- Parliament takes control of the army.
- The Nineteen Propositions.
- Charles declares war.

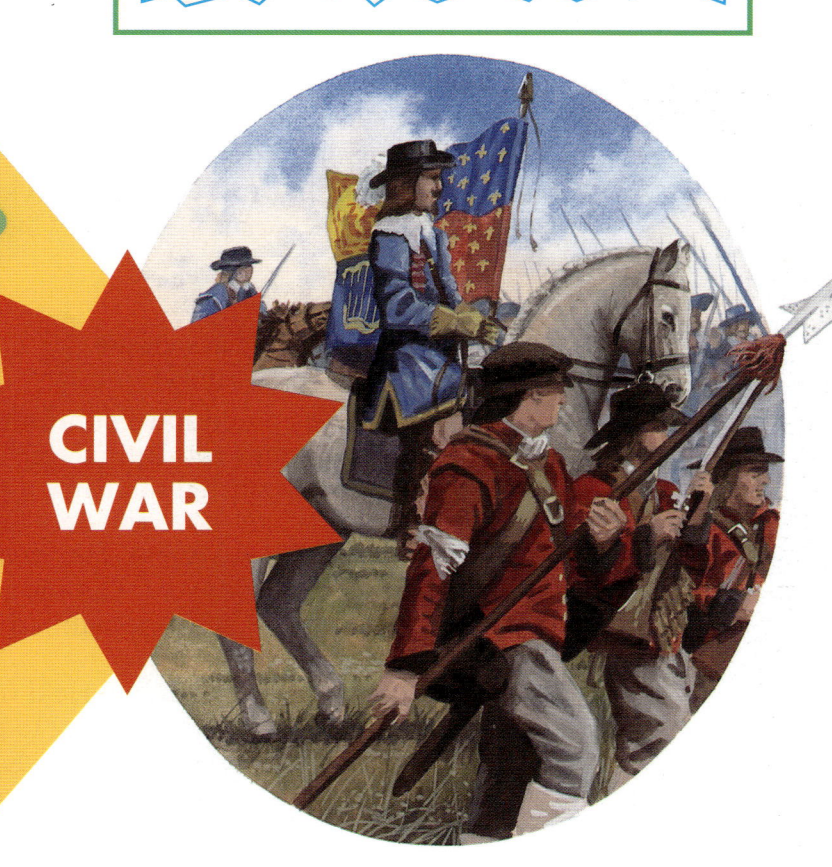

CIVIL WAR

WHY DID CIVIL WAR BREAK OUT IN 1642?

Close-up on Stage two

Charles I ruled without Parliament for eleven years. This was not unusual. Other monarchs had often ruled without Parliament in the past. But during this time Charles made some rather big mistakes.

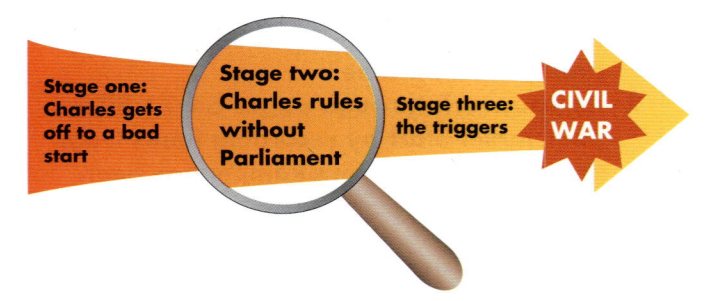

MONEY

Mistake 1: He introduced unpopular taxes

Now that Charles did not have a Parliament he had to find new ways to raise money.

One method he used was 'Ship Money'. This was a tax to improve the navy in times of war. It was usually paid only by counties on the coast and only in wartime. But, in 1635 and 1636 Charles demanded Ship Money from all counties even though there was no war. It looked as if Charles meant the tax to be permanent, paid every year. People who refused to pay were arrested.

RELIGION

Mistake 2: He tried to make the Church more Catholic

In the 1630s Charles began to make changes to the Church of England. He made churches more decorated. He discouraged the clergy from preaching sermons about the Bible.

These ideas upset a lot of people, particularly the extreme protestants known as the Puritans. Many thought he was trying to bring the Catholic Church back. Charles' wife was a Catholic and had her own chapel and priest. Perhaps Charles was also a Catholic!

Some Puritans wrote pamphlets attacking the Church and the monarchy. In 1637 Archbishop Laud put three Puritans who had written some of these pamphlets on trial. They were found guilty and punished severely (see Source 1).

MONEY AND RELIGION

Mistake 3: He tried to extend his policies into Scotland

Perhaps Charles could have continued to rule without Parliament. But in 1637 he did something which turned out to be a terrible mistake. He tried to make the Scots use the English Prayer Book. When they refused he sent an army to force them. But his army was beaten and the Scots demanded compensation.

Charles was in deep trouble. He'd run out of money. Taxpayers were refusing to pay their taxes. The only place he could get money was from Parliament. In the summer of 1640 he had to go back to Parliament to beg for their help. He seemed to be at their mercy. What would happen next?

▼ SOURCE 1

The executioner cut off Mr Burton's ears, deep and close, in a cruel manner with much bleeding, an artery being cut.

Mr Prynne's cheeks were seared with an iron made exceeding hot, after which the executioner cut off one of his ears and a piece of his cheek; then hacking the other ear almost off, left it hanging.

◀ **SOURCE 2** *Charles and his advisers are shown defending the tree of religion*

▼ ACTIVITY

1 Look at Sources 1–3. Were they written or drawn by supporters or opponents of Charles' religious policies? Explain your answer.
2 Add items from these two pages to your table.

▼ **SOURCE 3** *Archbishop Laud eating Puritans' ears for dinner*

WHY DID CIVIL WAR BREAK OUT IN 1642?

Compromise!
Charles now appeared to be at the mercy of Parliament. Nearly all the MPs in the House of Commons were united against him.

Yet, when Parliament met in November 1640, nobody dreamt that a civil war was close. The possibility was not in anyone's mind. In any case, there was nobody to fight on Charles' side. Almost everyone in Parliament agreed that Charles had to change his policies, and you need two sides to fight a war.

Parliament makes its demands in November 1640

We want you to:

- hold regular meetings of Parliament
- punish your ministers, especially Strafford, for the way they have behaved
- take advice from sensible ministers. Some of your ministers must come from Parliament.
- reverse the changes you and Archbishop Laud have made to the Church
- raise no more taxes without our agreement
- put an end to your special courts, such as the Court of Star Chamber, where you lock up your opponents without a trial.

▼ ACTIVITY

1 Compare Parliament's demands (page 66) with Charles' concessions (page 67). Which of Parliament's demands did Charles agree to?
2 Do you agree that by the summer of 1641 Parliament had got most of what it wanted?
3 Which of these statements do you agree with more?
   - These demands are revolutionary. They show that Parliament wanted to get rid of the King.
   - These demands show that Parliament was merely trying to get Charles to govern more sensibly.
4 Add items from these two pages to your table.

▼ DISCUSS

5 Was war inevitable by the summer of 1641? Explain your answer.

Charles gives in by the summer of 1641

- Parliament is to meet every three years and cannot be ended without MPs' agreement.
- Ship Money has been made illegal.
- The Court of the Star Chamber has been abolished.
- The Church reforms have **not** been reversed, but Archbishop Laud has been put in prison.
- Strafford, my minister who was hated most, has been tried by MPs and executed.

WHY DID CIVIL WAR BREAK OUT IN 1642?

Close-up on Stage three

Most historians agree that in the summer of 1641 nobody was even thinking civil war was possible. It looked as if the two sides had sorted out most of their differences.

Yet only twelve months later war began. The cartoons on this page explain why.

Stage one: Charles gets off to a bad start
Stage two: Charles rules without Parliament
Stage three: the triggers
CIVIL WAR

November 1641: Parliament demands more power

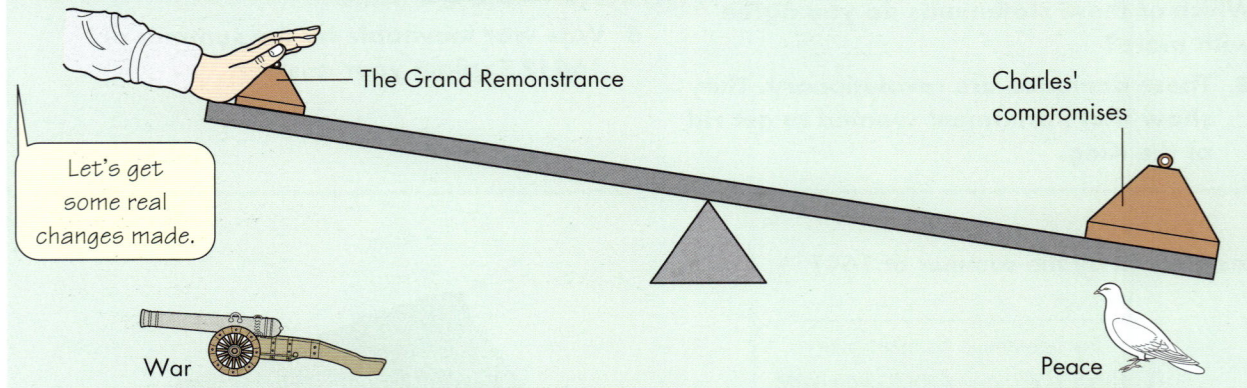

Let's get some real changes made.

The Grand Remonstrance — Charles' compromises

War — Peace

Extreme Puritan MPs made a new list of demands, called the Grand Remonstrance. For example, they demanded that:

- Parliament chose the King's ministers. This would give them power over how the country was run.
- the power of bishops be reduced. This would make the Church more Protestant.

MPs were divided about these demands: 159 voted for; 148 voted against. Charles was infuriated by the demands, but was encouraged by the divisions among MPs. He now seemed to have some support.

January 1642: Charles tries to arrest five MPs

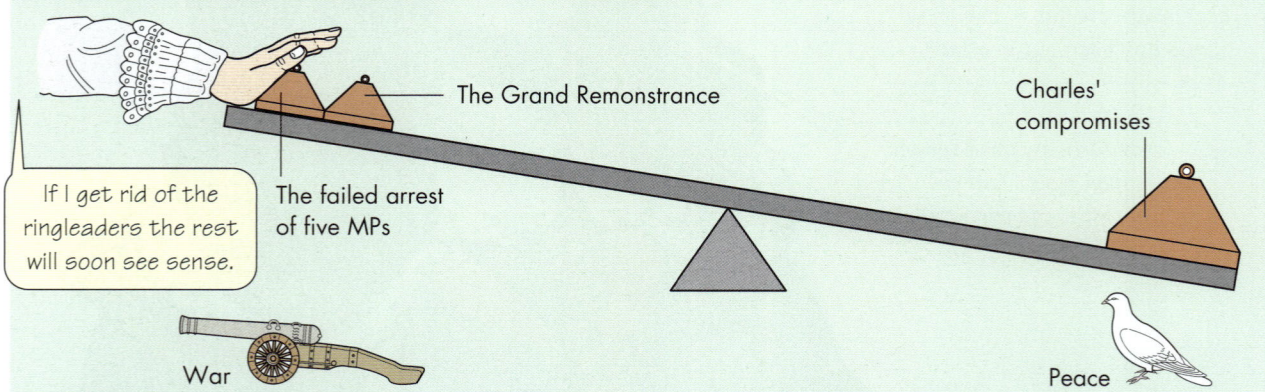

If I get rid of the ringleaders the rest will soon see sense.

The failed arrest of five MPs — The Grand Remonstrance — Charles' compromises

War — Peace

Many historians think that civil war was brought closer by Charles himself. MPs did not trust him. They feared he was planning to get rid of Parliament and rule by himself again. In January 1642 Charles did something which convinced MPs that this was what he was intending. Charles burst into the House of Commons with 400 soldiers and demanded that five leading MPs be handed over for arrest.

However, the MPs had been warned and had fled down the Thames by boat. They were protected by the Council of London and treated like heroes.

March 1642: Parliament takes control of the army

Labels on scales: Taking control of the army · The failed arrest of five MPs · The Grand Remonstrance · Charles' compromises

Speech bubble: If Charles has no army then he has no power.

War · Peace

England needed an army. Kings had always controlled the army in the past. But MPs did not trust Charles enough to let him have an army which he might use against them. So Parliament simply took control of the army without Charles' permission.

1 June 1642: the Nineteen Propositions – Parliament goes too far

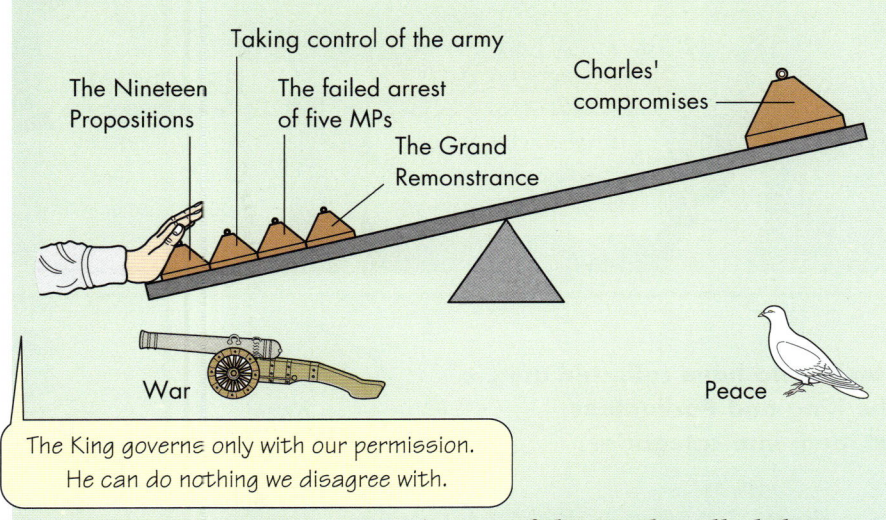

Labels on scales: The Nineteen Propositions · Taking control of the army · The failed arrest of five MPs · The Grand Remonstrance · Charles' compromises

War · Peace

Speech bubble: The King governs only with our permission. He can do nothing we disagree with.

On 1 June Parliament passed a set of demands called the Nineteen Propositions. This finally divided the King's supporters from his opponents.

▼ SOURCE 4 *Some of the Nineteen Propositions*

- All affairs of state, including foreign policy, religion and finance, must be agreed with Parliament.
- All ministers must be approved by Parliament.
- Parliament must control the education of the King's children. His children cannot marry without Parliament's approval.
- Laws against Catholics must be enforced.
- The Church must be reformed as Parliament wants.

▼ ACTIVITY

1. Add the final items to your table. There are quite a lot from these two pages.
2. Now it is time to look carefully at your tables.
   a) Which side do you think was most to blame for the bad relationship between the King and Parliament?
   b) Which side do you think was most to blame for the final slide into war?

▼ DISCUSS

3. Think back to your answer to Question 5 on page 67. At what point do you think civil war became inevitable?

Charles declares war

A lot of MPs thought the Nineteen Propositions went too far. Charles did too. He said they would make him 'a mere phantom of a king'. Charles' supporters left London to join him. Both sides got armies together. On 22 August Charles raised his standard at Nottingham. The Civil War had begun.

CIVIL WAR

WHY DID CIVIL WAR BREAK OUT IN 1642?

Money, religion and power

You will see from the work you have done so far in this section that a few arguments keep cropping up again and again. Let's look at them.

POWER

They shouldn't tell me what to do. I am the King! I am appointed by God.

MONEY

We should have a say in how the King spends his money.

POWER

He should not tell us what to do. We represent the people of England.

RELIGION

We must not let the King make England Catholic again.

▼ ACTIVITY A

1. Look again at your table. You should have collected quite a few points about the way the King and Parliament antagonised each other. Sort them into categories.

   Either:
   Colour code the points on your chart.
   - If they are to do with money, circle them in blue.
   - If they are to do with religion, circle them in yellow.
   - If they are to do with power, circle them in red.

   Some will be ringed in more than one colour.

   Or:
   Write each point on a separate slip of paper and then place them in the best place on a large diagram like the one on the right.

2. You are now going to write an essay about the causes of the Civil War. This is a difficult topic, but you have collected a lot of points for the essay on your table and there is a writing frame on the opposite page to help you further. You can also get some 'paragraph starters' from your teacher if you need them.

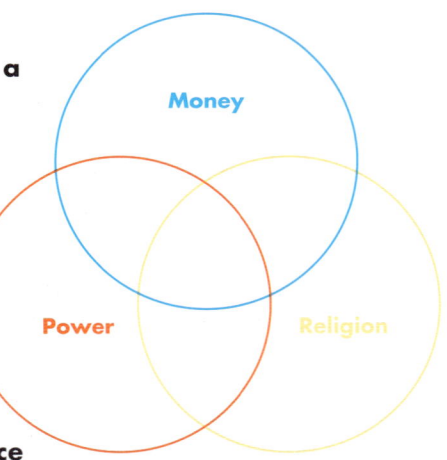

▼ **ACTIVITY B**

Work in pairs. Choose whether your pair is going to be on the King's side or Parliament's side.

It is August 1642. Civil war has broken out and two armies have gathered. You have been asked to prepare a poster or leaflet that will be displayed to all soldiers on your side. It must explain to the soldiers why they are fighting.

Mention whose fault the war is. Explain why your side is fighting. Back up your views with evidence from pages 62–70.

- If you are on the King's side, you will mainly be using the points in the right-hand column of your table. Point out how the Commons didn't know when to stop but kept on pushing for more and more concessions. They had to be stopped.
- If you are on Parliament's side, you will mainly be using the points in the left-hand column of your table. Point out how, at each stage, it was the King who made things worse. He first brought soldiers to Parliament. He declared war. He must be taught a lesson.

What caused the Civil War?

Introduction Explain when the Civil War started and that the main issues between the King and Parliament were power, money and religion.

Paragraph one: Money Look at the points you have made about the disagreements over money and write a few sentences about them.

Paragraph two: Religion Look at the points you have made about the disagreements over religion and write a few sentences about them. Mention how the King's actions antagonised the Protestants and how his policies in Scotland led to serious problems.

Paragraph three: Power Look at the points you have made about the disagreements over power and write a few sentences about them.

Paragraph four: Triggers Describe how the King's actions helped trigger the war. Then describe how the actions of Parliament helped trigger the war.

Conclusion Write a few sentences saying who you think was most to blame for the war.

What was life like during the Civil War?

▶▶ Civil wars are very nasty. Communities can be split so that people are fighting against former friends and neighbours. Members of the same family might even end up on different sides. Refugees flee from the fighting. Innocent people get caught in the crossfire.

You are now going to find out what life was like during the English Civil War. At the end of your enquiry you will write a short story about the war, and include some of the information you have discovered.

Who fought whom?

Some history books will give you a map like the one in Source 1 to show you who was on each side, but it is not quite as simple as that. In fact there are a lot of surprises.

What you would expect	What actually happened
All the rich gentry supported Charles	In fact, many gentry opposed Charles. In Lancashire, for example, 272 members of the gentry supported the King, 138 supported Parliament and nine changed sides during the war.
Most MPs supported Parliament	In fact, nearly half the MPs were on the King's side. And Charles' supporters were not just MPs from the south-east, but from all over the country.
Everyone took sides	In fact, between a third and two thirds of the gentry took no active part in the war. In 21 counties armies were organised to keep both sides out!
People chose sides on a matter of principle	In fact, many people did not choose which side they fought on. They tended to support the side whose army controlled their area or the side the local lord supported. Many gentry chose the side they thought would win.

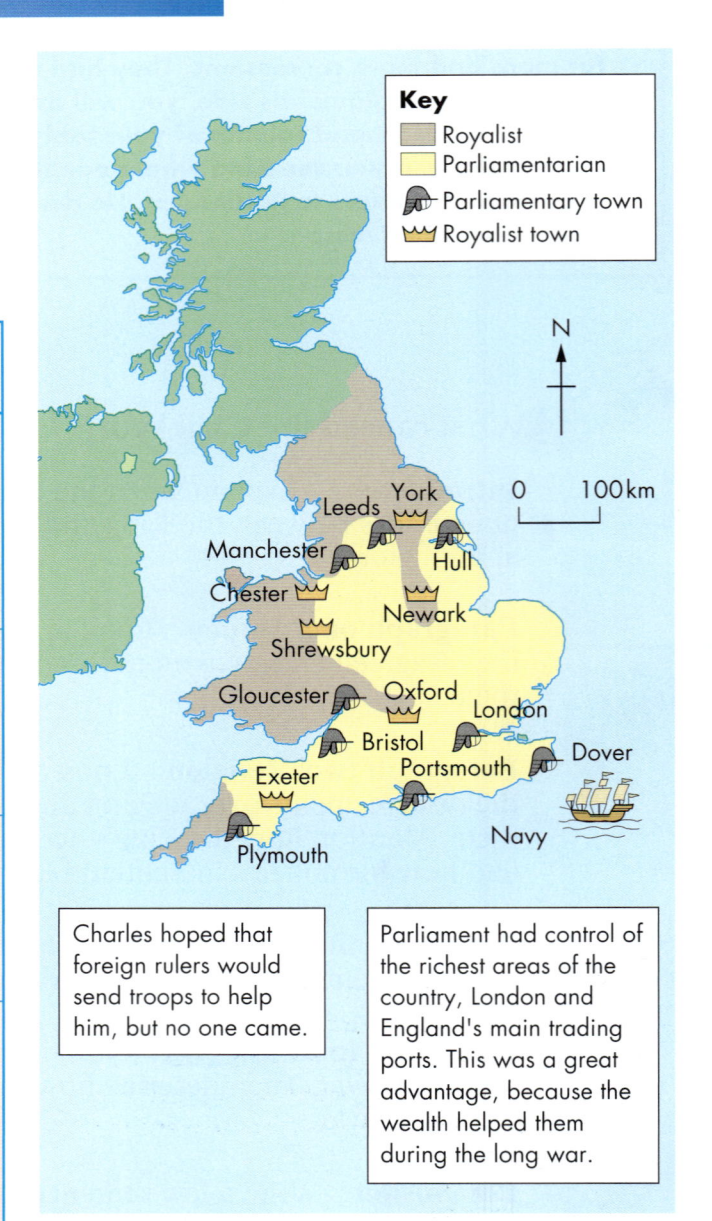

Charles hoped that foreign rulers would send troops to help him, but no one came.

Parliament had control of the richest areas of the country, London and England's main trading ports. This was a great advantage, because the wealth helped them during the long war.

▲ SOURCE 1

Fighting for the King: Royalists or 'Cavaliers'

Source 2 shows a Royalist soldier. He may not look like much of a soldier, but at the beginning the Royalists did much better in the fighting because they had better equipment and were used to guns. In fact, Charles might have been able to win the war early on, but he was too cautious and would not advance on London. Charles was not a good leader.

Fighting for Parliament: Parliamentarians or 'Roundheads'

Parliament did not really have a proper army at the start of the war. But Oliver Cromwell and Thomas Fairfax emerged as very good leaders. They formed and trained the New Model Army which was disciplined and well equipped. Source 3 shows a Parliamentarian soldier.

▲ SOURCE 2

▲ SOURCE 3

▼ ACTIVITY

1. Explain in your own words why the map in Source 1 is misleading.
2. On your own copy of Sources 2 and 3 label the following features. You will have to decide which of the two sources they apply to:

   - leather coat
   - iron back and breastplate
   - shoulder belt supporting a sword
   - left arm protected by an iron gauntlet
   - head protected by a 'pot' helmet
   - stand to support the musket when firing
   - charges of gunpowder
   - bullets in a round bag.

WHAT WAS LIFE LIKE DURING THE CIVIL WAR?

Case study one: plunder and violence

Innocent civilians were the greatest casualties of the Civil War. They were forced into fighting for one side or the other when all they wanted was to be able to get on with their lives. Villagers in Worcestershire were told that if they did not pay their taxes, 'Your houses will be pillaged and fired and your persons imprisoned.' Soldiers sent from the other side to protect towns went on the rampage themselves, looting houses and churches for food and valuables.

▶ **SOURCE 4** *From the title page of a pamphlet called* The Bloody Prince

▼ **SOURCE 5** *A print published during the war showing Royalist soldiers*

▲ **SOURCE 6** *Parliamentary soldiers in a church in 1646*

▼ **SOURCE 7** *A description of what Prince Rupert's troops did to Birmingham after capturing it in April 1643 (Rupert was Charles I's nephew)*

They ran into every house cursing and damning, threatening and terrifying the poor women most terribly, setting naked swords and pistols to their breasts. They fell to plundering all the town, picking purses and pockets, searching in holes and corners and every other place they could suspect for money or goods. They beastly assaulted many women's chastity, and bragged about it afterwards, how many they ravished.

The next day in every street they kindled fire with gunpowder, match, wisps of straw, hay and burning coals.

▼ **SOURCE 8** *'The Resolutions of the Clubmen of Dorset'*, 1645

We belong to an Association to preserve ourselves from plunder and violence.

Until we receive answers from the King and Parliament:

- The Constable of each town shall set a constant watch of two every night and they shall be well armed.
- All soldiers who are caught plundering shall be disarmed and returned to their army.
- If lodging is demanded by an army for a soldier he shall be friendly entertained if he behaves himself in his quarters.
- Any person assembling soldiers for the King or Parliament will not be given our protection.

▼ **ACTIVITY**

1. Look at Source 9. Can you see:
   - the goose instead of a musket
   - a dripping pan instead of a shield
   - bottles of wine hanging from his cross-belt
   - black pots instead of garters
   - an artichoke instead of a sword
   - a tripod pot and a duck on his head instead of a helmet?

2. Which of Sources 4–9 do you think were produced by:
   a) Royalists
   b) Parliamentarians
   c) neutrals?
   Explain how you made each decision.

3. Divide into pairs. One of you is a Royalist, the other a Parliamentarian. Each of you should design the front page of a pamphlet with words and a drawing showing how terrible the other side's soldiers are. Then compare your pamphlets.

▼ **DISCUSS**

4. What might civilians caught in a modern civil war think of Source 8?

▲ **SOURCE 9** *A contemporary caricature of a pillaging soldier*

WHAT WAS LIFE LIKE DURING THE CIVIL WAR?

Case study two: Lady Harley defends her castle

There were very few major battles in the Civil War, but there were a lot of sieges. Lady Brilliana Harley, and her husband, Sir Robert Harley, were Puritans and supporters of Parliament. Sir Robert was an MP and was in London with their son Ned during the years 1642–3. Lady Harley was left to defend her home, Brampton Castle in Herefordshire, as her neighbours turned against her and the Royalist forces moved closer.

Her letters to her son Ned show her worries during these two years. She had good reason to worry. When nearby Hopton Castle was taken by Royalists in 1644, the prisoners were tied up and laid on the ground so that their throats could be cut. The bodies were then thrown into a pit.

Here are extracts from Lady Harley's letters to her son Ned.

17 July 1642
I sent Samuel to Hereford to spy on the Royalists. He tells me all at Hereford cried out against your father.

19 July 1642
I long to see you, but would not have you come down, for I cannot think this country is very safe. I hope your father will give me full directions how I may best have the house guarded. My dear Ned, I thank God I am not afraid. It is the Lord's cause we stand for.

The boy I have sent to London is such a roguish boy that I dare not keep him in my house. I fear he will join the Royalists.

I have written to Worcester for 50 weight of shot. I sent to Worcester so I could keep it secret.

13 December 1642
I fear our corn and malt will not hold out if this continues; and they said they will burn my barns; and my fear is that they will place soldiers so near that there will be no going out.

28 January 1643
Mr Wigmore will not let the fowler bring me any fowl, nor will he let any of my servants pass — they dare not go to the town. They have forbidden my rents to be paid. We could be attacked by soldiers any day.

1 March 1643
I desire your father to send me word what he would have me do; if I dismiss my men I shall be plundered and if I have no rents, I know not what course to take. If I leave Brampton all will be ruined.

▼ ACTIVITY A

At this stage of the war Lady Harley starts to use a code in some of her letters. Your teacher can give you an example.

You are Lady Harley. Your code has been broken! Invent a new code and send one of Lady Harley's letters using your new code. See if the person sitting next to you can break your code.

After this Lady Harley stopped writing letters but another person in the castle continued.

26 July 1643
There appeared troops of horses facing our castle from a hill on the south side, and 300 foot soldiers to the east of our castle. Altogether there are 7900 enemy. The castle is manned by 50 musketeers.

27 July 1643
We fired all day with small shot on each other. They plundered our sheep and cattle.

3 August 1643
They began a fire in the town which had soon consumed nearly all the town. This evening they made ten shots against us, which only pierced our battlements but slew none of us so the power of God may be observed.

4 August 1643
Our parsonage and barns were burnt down.

9 August 1643
They planted five great guns against our castle as if they meant to have beaten it to dust.

15 August 1643
The enemy continued battering with their great gun from the church steeple, our worst friend.

9 September 1643
The Lord was this day pleased to take away these bloody villains. Our food had nearly run out, the roof of the castle was so battered that there was not one dry room, yet this noble lady bore all with admirable patience.

In October 1643 the attackers returned and the great guns began to batter the castle once more. Lady Harley held out again, but then died of a bad cold. The defenders surrendered early in 1644.

▼ ACTIVITY B

1. Write out a list of examples of Lady Harley's bravery.
2. Write out a list of all the different methods and weapons used by the Royalists to besiege and attack Brampton Castle.
3. What evidence can you find that the people in the castle were sure God was on their side?
4. You are a Royalist soldier. In no more than 100 words describe the main events that took place at Brampton Castle between July 1642 and September 1643. Remember that the accounts you have read were written by people inside the castle. You must write your account from the point of view of a Royalist outside the castle.

WHAT WAS LIFE LIKE DURING THE CIVIL WAR?

Case study three: And when did you last see your father?

Source 10 shows a scene from the Civil War. We do not know who the boy and girl are. But it is clear that they have been captured by the enemy. The boy is being questioned. Soon his sister will be questioned too.

▲ **SOURCE 10** *A nineteenth-century painting called 'And when did you last see your father?'*

▼ DISCUSS

1 Discuss the scene shown in Source 10.
   a) Who are the Royalists and who are the Parliamentarians? How do you know?
   b) What can you work out about the boy and the girl's family? Are they rich or poor?
   c) Why do you think the men are looking for the children's father?
   d) Who is asking the questions?
   e) What are the other people in the picture doing?
   f) How do you think the children were captured?
   g) What will the boy say to the question 'And when did you last see your father?'
   h) What other questions will the man ask?
   i) Are the boy and girl afraid?
   j) What do you think will happen next?

▼ ACTIVITY

2 You are now going to write your own story, using Source 10 as your starting point or end point.

   ■ If you use it as your starting point think about what will happen next.
   ■ If you use it as your end point think about the events that have led to this moment.
   ■ Try to use the ideas and information that you have found out about life during the Civil War in your story.
   ■ Follow this recipe:

   a) Your story should only include three characters: either the boy or the girl, either the father or the mother, and a soldier.
   b) It should take place in a single 24-hour period.
   c) All the action should take place in the family's house or garden.

Why did the English execute their King?

> In 1648, Parliament put the King on trial for treason. Then they executed him. Over the next four pages you will explore why they did this and why it was such an earth-shattering thing to do.

The background

Parliament won a decisive victory at the Battle of Naseby in 1645. It became clear to the King whose army was best. Charles knew he could not win. He surrendered in 1646. He was imprisoned in Carisbrooke Castle on the Isle of Wight.

But while Charles was in Carisbrooke Castle negotiating with Parliament, he secretly persuaded the Scots to invade England. The Royalists were easily defeated, but many people were killed. Parliament no longer trusted Charles and decided he had to be put on trial.

The trial

The trial was fixed for 20 January 1649, in Westminster Hall. Many people on Parliament's side were very reluctant to be involved in the trial. After all, it was a big thing putting a king on trial! Many top lawyers and judges disappeared to their country estates to escape being involved. A High Court Justice was set up, made up of 135 commissioners, who were really both judges and jury. But on the first day only 68 of the 135 turned up!

Charles was brought before the court. The charges against him were read out by John Bradshaw, the President of the Court. But Charles refused to accept them. He claimed that the court was unlawful, that a king could not be tried by his people. He argued that the court had no authority.

Things were not going according to Parliament's plan! But they could not give up. That would be like admitting that they had no power to try Charles. John Bradshaw ordered that Charles be removed. The trial then continued in his absence.

The charges

Charles was trusted with a limited power to govern according to the laws of the land and to use this power for the good of the people. But he has:

- overthrown the rights and liberties of the people
- taken away the power of Parliament
- made war against Parliament and the people.

Charles Stuart is guilty of all the treasons, murders, burnings, and mischiefs to this nation committed in the wars.

Charles' defence

I demand to know by what power I am called here? By what lawful authority? Remember, I am your King, your lawful King. Think about these things before you go from one sin to an even greater one. I have a trust committed to me by God, by lawful inheritance. I will not give it up to answer to a new and unlawful authority.

▼ ACTIVITY

You are going to hold a trial to decide whether Charles I was guilty of the charges brought against him.

1. Get into groups and decide whether you are going to prepare the case for the prosecution or the case for the defence.
2. Look at the charges on page 80. Then look at the beginning of each of the eight witness statements below. Decide which can help your case.
3. Look back over pages 62–79 to help you add to or complete the witness statements. Your teacher can give you some extra help or some complete witness statements if you need them.
4. You can use your own research to add other witnesses.
5. You should think about how you are going to challenge what the other side's witnesses have to say.
6. a) To carry out the trial you will need:
   - John Bradshaw, President of the Court
   - the commissioners
   - the prosecution
   - the defence
   - the witnesses
   - Charles – or an empty chair to represent him.

   b) The prosecution makes its case first, then the defence. Each side can question the other side's witnesses.

   c) Take a vote to see if your class thinks the case against the King has been proved.

Gentlemen, you have no right to sit in judgement on our King. Kings are . . .

It was not the King who caused the war. It was Parliament itself by . . .

I was the King's servant. He is a kind, loving and generous man who looks after all who work for him. I respect him. He always . . .

My lords, I come here today to plead for reason. This war did no good for the ordinary people of England. Nor will this trial. We should . . .

I heard Charles say to one of his officers who was mistreating prisoners, 'I do not care if you cut them three times more, for they are my enemies.' As Commander of his army Charles is responsible for what his soldiers did. They . . .

I was present in the House of Commons on 4 January 1642 when the King tried to arrest five of my fellow MPs. The King caused the war. He . . .

Parliament did not declare war on the King. The King declared war on Parliament. I was there in . . .

I caught Elizabeth Stiles carrying this letter from Charles to his supporters in Scotland. It says . . .

WHY DID THE ENGLISH EXECUTE THEIR KING?

The sentence

On 27 January 1649, Charles I was brought before the court. He was found guilty. The court said that it was the duty of the King to see that Parliaments were called frequently and Charles had not done this.

The sentence was read out. The King was 'to be put to death by the severing of his head from his body'.

The commissioners were extremely nervous about signing the death warrant. Only about 40 of them signed without hesitation; the others had to be forced to sign it. In the end only 52 out of the original 135 actually signed the death warrant.

The execution

On the morning of 30 January Charles rose early. He asked for two shirts. It was cold and he did not want to appear to be shivering from fear. He was then taken to Whitehall, where he ate a piece of bread and drank some wine and then prayed. At two o'clock he stepped onto the scaffold.

▼ **SOURCE 1** *From the diaries of Philip Henry, who was visiting his father in London at the time*

I stood amongst the crowd where the scaffold was erected, and saw what was done, but was not so near as to hear anything. I saw the blow given, I can truly say, with a sad heart. At that instant, I remember well, there was such a groan by the thousands then present, as I never heard before and desire I may never hear again. There was according to order one troop immediately marching from Charing Cross to Westminster and another from Westminster to Charing Cross, purposely to massacre the people, and to disperse and scatter them, so that I had much trouble amongst the rest to escape home without hurt.

▼ **SOURCE 2** *A contemporary picture of Charles' execution, by a Dutch artist*

Afterwards, devoted followers of the King and souvenir hunters rushed to dip their handkerchiefs in his blood and to take hairs from his head and beard. The following day his head was sewn back on, and a few days later the body was quietly buried at Windsor Castle.

▼ **SOURCE 3** *The execution of Charles, painted by a French contemporary*

▼ ACTIVITY

1. Source 2 shows three separate events taking place on the scaffold. What are they?
2. Describe the different reactions of the people marked A, B and C in Sources 2 and 3.
3. What evidence is there that the painter of Source 3 may have seen Source 2?
4. Why do you think Dutch and French artists were interested in painting this event?
5. Do you think these sources taken together give us reliable evidence about:
   - where the execution took place
   - who was on the scaffold
   - who was in the crowd
   - whether there were soldiers there
   - how the spectators reacted?

▼ DISCUSS

6. What evidence is there that Parliament was very nervous about the trial and the execution?
7. Why do you think Parliament wanted to try Charles?
8. Why do you think Parliament wanted to execute Charles?
9. Do you think the trial and the execution were necessary?

Why did they want the King back?

▶▶ 'Help! What do we do now?' The big problem after the execution of Charles I was how to govern England without a king. Kings and queens had ruled for centuries and people did not really know how to run a country without one. Over the next eight pages you will see the different methods they tried and why, eleven years after Charles' head was chopped off, his son Charles II was invited to come back and be King!

The world turned upside down

◀ **SOURCE 1**
The word turned upside down – a cartoon drawn in 1647 by 'a well-wisher to the King'

After the Civil War new and extreme ideas about how society should be organised began to circulate.

A few years earlier this would not have been allowed. But people were now freer to say what they liked. Anyone with a printing press could publish pamphlets. These new ideas were only supported by a small number of people at the time, but many – gentry, MPs and ordinary people, too – felt very threatened by them.

The Diggers
Diggers believed:

- that 'no one branch of mankind should rule over another'
- that God made land for everyone to share. It should not just be owned by the rich.

A group of Diggers occupied the common land at St George's Hill, Surrey. They said that if everyone did this there would be an end to hunger and poverty.

Share out the land

The Levellers

The Levellers wanted:

Power to the people

- Parliament to run the country and MPs to be elected by all men over the age of 21 (except servants, those who received poor relief and those who fought for the King during the Civil War)
- trial by jury
- freedom for people to worship how they wished
- the death penalty only for murder.

The Levellers had a great deal of support amongst soldiers in the New Model Army. The army was very powerful at this time, which worried the government.

Fifth Monarchists

Get England ready for Jesus

The Fifth Monarchists believed Christ was about to win his struggle with the devil and would soon come down to earth. Their job was to make earth a fit place for Christ to visit. Many of them were London cloth merchants and craftsmen.

- They disliked the gentry and refused to take their hats off or bow down to those higher up in society.
- They did not believe in being governed by elected MPs. They wanted a Parliament of godly people to run the country.
- They wanted to change the legal system. For example they wanted thieves to work for the people they stole from instead of being hanged.

Women

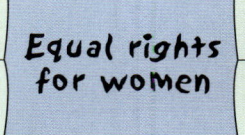

Equal rights for women

All these other groups were dominated by men. In 1649 a group of women petitioned Parliament.

▼ SOURCE 2
The women's petition

We desire a share in the freedoms of this state. Have we not an equal interest with the men of this nation? Are our lives, rights or goods to be taken from us more than from men? And can you imagine us to be so stupid as not to see when [our rights] are being daily broken down?

▼ ACTIVITY

1. Look at Source 1.
   a) List all the things that are 'wrong'.
   b) Explain what the artist was saying when he drew the picture.
   c) Why is it important to know that the artist is a 'well-wisher to the King'?
2. Make two lists showing the ideas put forward by the four groups. One list should contain the ideas that would be accepted today, and the other list the ideas that would not be.

▼ DISCUSS

3. How do you think Parliament dealt with each group? Your teacher can tell you if you are right.

▼ EXTRA

4. Despite the Civil War England was still run by the gentry and the middle classes who owned land or property and were well off. Imagine you are the man in the picture, a member of the gentry in the 1650s. Write a speech bubble to explain:
   a) why you do not like the ideas of the various groups described on these two pages
   b) which group worries you most and why
   c) what Parliament should do about the groups.

WHY DID THEY WANT THE KING BACK?

Who were the Puritans?

You have met the Puritans before. They were extreme Protestants. Puritans believed in a simple religion and a simple lifestyle – they dressed plainly and believed you had to work hard if you wanted to go to Heaven when you died. They also believed that Sunday was the most important day of the week, and that on Sundays and other holy days people should devote themselves entirely to God. Source 3 was drawn by the Puritans to show what they thought people should and shouldn't do on Sundays.

▲ **SOURCE 3** *An engraving made by Puritans in 1639*

The Puritans on top

Since the 1600s the strength of the Puritans had been growing. They were no longer a minority. Now the Civil War was over, the Puritans in Parliament had the upper hand. Some Puritans saw this as their opportunity to force the Puritan religion and way of life on the people of England. They could force everyone to live a godly, sinless life – whether they were Puritan or not. In some areas the Puritans had already passed local laws banning sinful pursuits. Now they tried to enforce Puritan ways all over the country.

Horse-racing, cock-fighting and bear-baiting were forbidden.

All theatres were closed. No games or sports were allowed on Sundays. Even going for a walk for any reason other than going to church was outlawed.

Gambling dens and brothels were closed.

The number of alehouses was reduced.

▼ ACTIVITY

1 Look at Source 3. The Puritans called the pictures on one side 'the works of light' and the ones on the other side 'the works of darkness'. Describe what is happening in each scene, then copy and complete the table below to show what the Puritans liked and disliked.

'Works of light' (Things the Puritans thought you should do on Sunday)	'Works of darkness' (Things the Puritans thought you should not do on Sunday)

▼ EXTRA

2 Write a speech bubble for this ordinary man who enjoys a drink and a bit of fun. What might he say about the things the Puritans were doing?

It looked as if the Puritans were determined to stop people enjoying themselves. In some parts of the country the laws were not seriously enforced because people objected to them so much. In other areas they were very strictly enforced.

WHY DID THEY WANT THE KING BACK?

'The most powerful man in England'

The bitter Civil War had torn England apart. The real power in England was with the army. As the leader of the army, Oliver Cromwell was the most powerful person in England at the end of the war. Ideas about how England should be governed therefore revolved around him.

Oliver Cromwell

Before the war Cromwell had been a Puritan MP – but not a leading one. During the Civil War he became the leader of the New Model Army, through sheer ability. He was a clever and brave commander and a strong wartime leader.

Oliver Cromwell was very religious. He felt that God was on his side. However, unlike some other Puritans, he wanted people to be free to worship as they chose.

Idea one: give MPs the power

Everyone expected a lot from Parliament once the King had gone. After all, the war had been all about giving real power to Parliament.

Problem: Parliament did very little. The MPs made Cromwell angry because they seemed more concerned with limiting religious freedom than sorting out the country. MPs abolished Christmas and closed all the theatres, but they refused to hold new elections.

Result: Cromwell got so frustrated with Parliament that he marched into the House of Commons with his soldiers and threw the MPs out.

Cromwell acted just like the old King did!

Idea two: give Cromwell the power

In 1653 a new Parliament established a new Constitution. It made Cromwell Lord Protector. He was now ruler of England, but he had to work with a council which was chosen by Parliament and he had to call Parliament regularly.

Problem: Cromwell could not get on with Parliament. They argued over religion.

Result: Cromwell dismissed Parliament in 1655.

This man is too powerful!

Idea four: make Cromwell King

Many people thought that the only way to bring back law and order was to bring back the monarchy. They did not want Charles' son to become Charles II, so in 1657 they asked Oliver Cromwell to become King!

Problem: Cromwell turned down the kingship because the army would not support him. However, he did agree that his son would become Lord Protector after he died, just as the son of a king became king when his father died.

Result: On 3 September 1658 Cromwell died of pneumonia. His son reluctantly became Lord Protector.

It seems to me that Cromwell has more power than Charles had!

Idea three: give the army the power

Cromwell did not want the army to run England, but everyone was running out of alternatives. Cromwell divided the country up into eleven districts, each one ruled by a Major-General from the army.

Why can't he just let people have some fun?

Problem: The Major-Generals were very unpopular. Puritan soldiers ruined people's fun. For example, they stopped horse-races and plays and they banned dancing on May Day.

Result: Cromwell got a very bad reputation. People did not like being ruled by the army. The gentry did not like paying taxes for the upkeep of the soldiers. Riots broke out. After two years Cromwell ended the experiment and got rid of the Major-Generals.

Idea five: bring the King back

In May 1659 the army forced Cromwell's son out of his job as Lord Protector and he returned to being a farmer. In 1660, the army – with the agreement of most MPs and ordinary people – decided they wanted a King back. The old one wasn't available – he'd been executed – but his son was. So, he was invited to become Charles II. He accepted and England had a King once more.

▼ EXTRA

Write a speech bubble for a Cromwell critic. What might he say about the decision to bring the King back?

WHY DID THEY WANT THE KING BACK?

Two views of Oliver Cromwell

Oliver Cromwell is one of the most important figures in English history. But opinion about him is divided. Was he a hero, who guided England through a difficult time, or a tyrant, who grabbed power for himself? Sources 4–6 give very different impressions of Cromwell. See if you can work out what they are saying about him.

> ### ▼ ACTIVITY A
> 1. Look at Sources 5 and 6. Which is pro-Cromwell and which is anti? How do you know?
> 2. Which view of Cromwell do you most agree with? Explain why.

▶ **SOURCE 4** *An engraving called 'Cromwell between the Pillars'*

Look at Source 6.
1. Where is Cromwell?
2. Who appears to be driving the horses?
3. Who has been run over?
4. Why are the three women weeping?

▼ **SOURCE 5** *Written by Bishop Burnet 50 years after the events*

Cromwell would rather have taken a shepherd's staff than the Protectorship. Nothing went more against his feelings than a show of greatness. But he saw it was necessary at that time, to keep the nation from falling into extreme disorder.

◀ **SOURCE 6** *An engraving called 'Cromwell's chariot'*

▼ **ACTIVITY B**

Why did so many people want the King back again?

1 The first stage in answering this question is to review some of the work you have done so far. Think about the following questions, but do not write anything.
   a) Look back at page 84. Which powerful group of people was worried by the new ideas?
   b) Look back at page 87. Which groups of people were unhappy about the things the Puritans did?
   c) Look at pages 88–89. What problems were there in trying to find a way to govern the country?

2 It is now time to organise your ideas. Look at the people below. Write a few sentences to explain why each of them might have welcomed the King back. You will already have ideas for three of them from Question 1.

An MP

An ordinary man

A soldier in the New Model Army

A member of the gentry

A Catholic who supported Charles during the Civil War

The same old story?

▶▶ **Now for a breathless sprint through thirty years of English history. See if you can keep up.**

1 The return of the King Charles II was crowned King in 1660. All the laws passed between 1641 and 1660 were declared illegal. The Church of England was brought back. Bishops were appointed. Cromwell's main supporters were punished.

2 Freedom Life after the 'Restoration' was more enjoyable. Theatres were reopened. There was a wave of new plays, music and poetry written.

3 Help – he's a Catholic! Charles had some arguments with Parliament, but he tried to avoid his father's mistakes. He kept quiet about religion. Then, on his death bed, he admitted to being a Catholic. And his heir, his brother James, was definitely a Catholic. Oh no!

4 Rebellion! A group of Protestants tried to overthrow James II. James had 250 of them executed and 1000 were sold to the West Indies as slaves. These harsh punishments were not popular.

5 James II makes more mistakes Without Parliament's permission James allowed Catholics to worship as they wished. He also appointed Catholic army officers, which was against the law. He built up a large army. People worried that the old troubles were returning. Would all this lead to another civil war?

6 Where did the baby come from? The Protestants had one big hope: James was old and did not have a son. After he died they would be able to choose a Protestant King. Then suddenly it was announced that the Queen had given birth to a son. This meant that the next King would be a Catholic. Stories spread that the baby was not hers, but had been smuggled into the palace in a warming pan (a pan usually filled with coals to warm the bed).

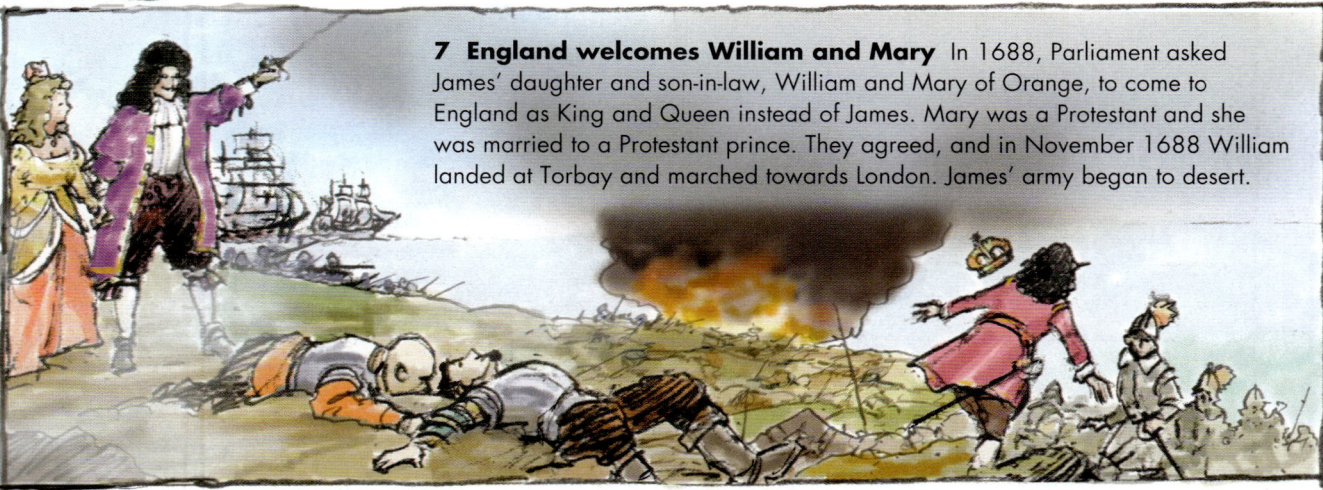

7 England welcomes William and Mary In 1688, Parliament asked James' daughter and son-in-law, William and Mary of Orange, to come to England as King and Queen instead of James. Mary was a Protestant and she was married to a Protestant prince. They agreed, and in November 1688 William landed at Torbay and marched towards London. James' army began to desert.

9 The events of 1688 have been called the 'Glorious Revolution'. England got rid of an unpopular monarch and replaced him with one they had chosen without a war.

The Glorious Revolution

8 Let him go! James lost his nerve and tried to escape to France, but his boat was shipwrecked. He was rescued by some fishermen who sent him back to London. William ordered that James be 'allowed to escape' again. James fled to France, just as William had wanted him to.

▼ ACTIVITY

1 On a piece of paper, draw or describe a picture that might go in each of the empty frames in the story (frames 6 and 8).

▼ DISCUSS

2 Why do you think William wanted James to escape?

Review: A different kind of monarchy

▼ **REVIEW ACTIVITY**

William and Mary became King and Queen under certain conditions. After 1688, monarchs in England were no longer as powerful as they had been before.

1 Look at the two pictures and decide which of them the following captions apply to:

- 'Chosen' by God
- Cannot suspend laws
- Cannot raise taxes without Parliament's consent
- Is a Catholic
- Controls the army
- Must call Parliament every three years
- 'Chosen' by Parliament
- Can rule without Parliament
- Cannot be a Catholic
- Cannot have an army in peacetime
- Rules with help from ministers

2 Choose the two most important changes that happened to the monarchy between 1500 and 1700. Give reasons for your choice.

3 Which of the following statements do you most agree with?

- In 1500 the King had all the power and in 1700 Parliament had all the power.
- Between 1500 and 1700 there was a shift in power in Parliament's favour but the monarch was still quite powerful.

SECTION 4

HOW MODERN WAS BRITAIN IN THE 1700s?

The picture shows a scientific experiment in the mid-1700s. What do you think is happening?

This picture might suggest to you that Britain was now a modern country full of clever, scientific-minded people. See if you agree as you find out about Britain in the 1700s.

A Scientific Revolution?

>> The changes that took place in the seventeenth century have been called a 'Scientific Revolution'. Is this a good description? On pages 96–97 you will look at some 'Yes!' evidence, and on pages 98–99 you will look at some 'No!' evidence.

SCIENTIFIC YES! REVOLUTION

1500

This is how an educated man might have thought in 1500.

> God controls everything that happens in the world. He even controls the weather. When there is a good harvest that is God's will. When there is a bad harvest that is God's will too.

> The Earth is the centre of the universe. The Sun, the Moon and the stars are fixed to great crystal spheres which circle the Earth.

> The best way of finding out how our bodies work is to read the medical books written by Galen hundreds of years ago. Our bodies contain four 'humours' – blood, phlegm, yellow bile and black bile. We get ill when these four humours get out of balance. The cure is to get them back in balance. For instance, if an illness is caused by too much blood, the answer is to bleed the patients to remove the extra blood.

1750

Over the next two centuries people became much more interested in observing the world and in doing scientific experiments. They wanted to find out if what people had thought in the past was actually true.

▼ ACTIVITY A

Look at the picture above. Now copy and complete the word bubbles for the picture below which shows the same scene 250 years later, in 1750. You must assume the man is educated and understands the latest scientific developments. You can get all the information you need from the timeline on page 97.

> It is not God who decides what happens, it is . . .

> The Earth is . . .

> The best ways of finding out how our bodies work is to . . .

PRINCIPIA

1500 The printing press was introduced to Britain. This made it easier for scientists to read about the latest scientific discoveries.

1543 In Italy, Vesalius, a doctor, published accurate drawings of the human body.

▶ **SOURCE 1**
One of Vesalius' drawings. He insisted that every doctor should do dissections himself to learn about the human body

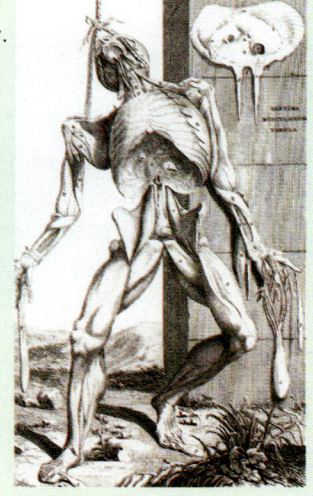

1698 The first steam engine was developed by Thomas Savery to pump water from tin mines in Cornwall.

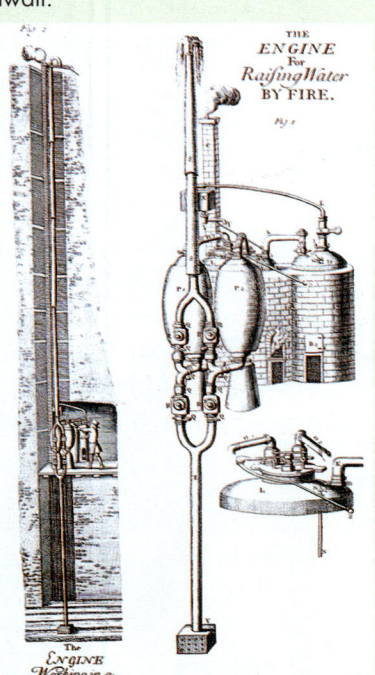

▲ **SOURCE 2** *Savery's mine pump*

1500
1550
1600
1650
1700
1750

▼ **ACTIVITY B**
Look at the scientific developments shown on this page. Choose a development that would:
- make people more healthy
- help scientists understand the world
- help industry.

1610 In Italy, Galileo showed that the Earth was not at the centre of the Universe. He proved that the Earth goes round the Sun.

1628 In London, William Harvey proved that the blood circulates continuously around the body. Doctors began to experiment with blood transfusions.

1661 In London, Boyle used air pumps to discover that air is essential for breathing and for burning.

1662 Scientists met to share their discoveries. One important group which started in Britain in 1662 was called the Royal Society.

1680s New mechanical looms were introduced that could weave cloth four times faster than hand looms.

1686 In London, Isaac Newton published his *Principia*, the most important scientific book yet written. It showed that there were natural laws such as gravity which kept the Universe going.

1717 Lady Mary Wortley introduced the smallpox inoculation to Britain. A test was made on six orphans, and when they survived the King's grandchildren were successfully inoculated.

A SCIENTIFIC REVOLUTION?

The witch hunts

Now for the other side of the coin. Some people may have been interested in science but others were more interested in superstition. A pamphlet about witch hunts sold thousands more copies than a pamphlet on science.

Look at Source 5. It is 1612 and Mary Sutton has been accused of being a witch. Her hands have been tied together in the shape of a cross. She is being lowered into the water. The people accusing her say that if she sinks she is innocent, if she floats she is guilty.

In the Middle Ages people thought a lot about Heaven and Hell, but they were not really worried about witches. Then, in the sixteenth and seventeenth centuries, people started finding witches everywhere. Just as God had priests to do his work, so people believed the devil also had 'servants' – called witches. The devil used his witches to bring all sorts of trouble to good Christians. Witches could make their victims fall ill or die, and they could harm crops and cattle.

King James I was very interested in witchcraft. In 1590 he wrote a book on the subject and suggested ways to identify a witch. One way is shown in Source 5. He said that another way to recognise a witch was by a mark on the witch's body, because at night the devil would come and visit the witch in the form of a pet and suck the witch's blood.

Laws were passed that allowed witches to be tried in the courts. In 1604 witchcraft became a crime punishable by death. There were more cases of witchcraft in the Essex courts than of any other crime, apart from theft. Hundreds of witches were hanged all around Britain – the last one as late as 1727. And for every case that came to court, there were many more accusations of witchcraft in villages that never got to court. Most of the people accused were old women.

Anyone could accuse anyone else of 'bewitching' them. Anything that went wrong in your life – from a sick cow to the death of a child – could be blamed on witchcraft. The most ridiculous accusations were believed.

SCIENTIFIC NO! REVOLUTION

▼ **SOURCE 3** *Extracts from the trial and confession of Joan Williford in 1645*

About seven years ago the devil did appear to Joan Williford in the shape of a little dog. He asked her to give up God and turn to him instead. The devil promised her money.

She called the devil 'Bunnie'. She said Bunnie pushed Thomas Graddler out of the window and into the cesspool.

She gave some of her blood to the devil, who promised to serve her for twenty years. Since she has been in prison she has seen the devil twice. He has tried to suck her. The devil came to her disguised as a mouse.

▼ **SOURCE 4** *An examination of a witch in Newcastle in 1649*

He laid her body naked to the waist, with her clothes over her head. With fright and shame all her blood ran to one part of her body. He run a pin into her thigh, and suddenly let her clothes fall and asked her why she did not bleed. Then he took out the pin and set her aside as a child of the devil.

◀ **SOURCE 5** *A contemporary engraving of the 'trial' of Mary Sutton*

▲ **SOURCE 6** *A seventeenth-century woodcut of a witch. She is standing by a magic circle, making a spell to summon the devil*

▲ **SOURCE 8** *A witch creating a storm at sea. Stories of witchcraft trials were very popular. The new printing presses made money out of selling pamphlets like this telling the latest sensational witchcraft stories. Sources 6–8 all come from such pamphlets*

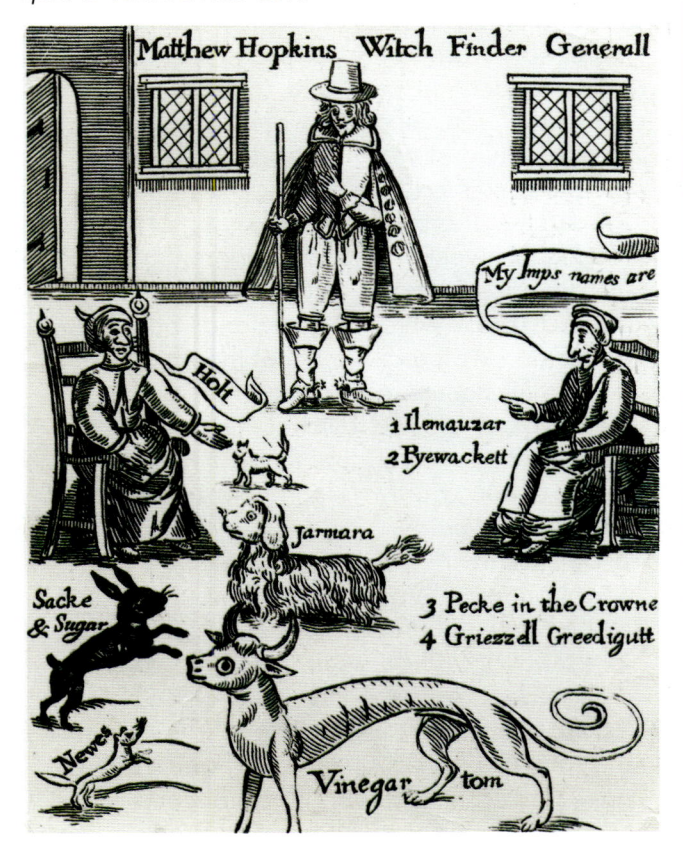

▲ **SOURCE 7** *Matthew Hopkins, Witchfinder General. He has accused the two women of being witches. The devil was supposed to have come to them disguised as the animals with strange names*

▼ ACTIVITY A

1. Look at Sources 4 and 5. They both show or describe methods of trying witches. Were these methods fair?
2. Look at Sources 3, 6 and 8. Why do you think people were ready to believe stories such as these?

▼ EXTRA

3. Witch-hunters were paid £1 for every witch they discovered. Design an advert for the job of witch-hunter.

▼ ACTIVITY B

4. Write a paragraph on each of the following:
   a) the reasons why the 'Scientific Revolution' is a good description for the period 1500–1750. You can get lots of ideas from pages 96–97.
   b) the reasons why 'an age of superstition' is a good description for this period. You can get lots of ideas from pages 98–99.
   c) the reasons why it is important for historians to look at a wide range of evidence before reaching conclusions.

How did London change?

>> In 1500 London was already a large city – by far the largest in Britain. By 1750 it had trebled in size. The skyline had changed beyond recognition. And it had become one of the biggest and busiest cities in Europe. In this enquiry you are going to look at some of the big changes.

The Plague: 'what a sad time it is'

Sixteenth-century London was a very unhealthy place. The buildings were made of wood and plaster and were built so close to each other that it was possible to walk around large parts of London on the rooftops. There had been no street planning when the houses were built and the city was a chaotic maze of streets and buildings. There was also no sewage system. Water came from the rivers and streams.

There were some grand palaces owned by the very rich and a few big houses built by prosperous merchants, but most houses were squalid and cramped.

To make matters worse, London was frequently hit by the Plague. Nearly 40,000 people (a quarter of the population) died in 1563, and another 25,000 died in both 1603 and 1625.

Londoners were used to regular visits from the Plague, but in 1665 one of the worst epidemics ever broke out and 80,000 people died.

Source 2 describes one person's view of what life was like in London during the Plague of 1665.

▼ **SOURCE 2** *Extracts from Samuel Pepys' diary for 1665*

7 June This day I did in Drury Lane see two or three houses marked with a red cross upon the doors and 'Lord Have Mercy Upon Us' writ there. This worried me so much that I bought a roll of tobacco to smell and chew.

29 June Travelled by water to Whitehall, where the Court was full of waggons and people ready to leave town.

20 July There were 1089 dying of the Plague this week. My Lady Carteret did give me a bottle of plague water.

12 August My Lord commands people to be inside by nine at night that the sick may leave their homes for air and exercise.

31 August 6102 died of the Plague this week. But it is feared that the true number is near 10,000, partly from the poor that cannot be taken notice of.

3 September Dared not wear my new wig, bought in Westminster where the Plague is. Nobody will dare buy any hair for fear of infection, that it had been cut off the heads of people dead from the Plague.

20 September But, Lord! What a sad time it is to see no boats on the river, and the grass grows all up and down Whitehall court and nobody but poor wretches in the streets.

▲ **SOURCE 1** *A plague doctor's uniform protected him from catching the Plague*

- Leather hat
- Mask with glass eyes and a beak stuffed with perfume or spices
- Stick to drive people away
- Leather gloves
- Gown of waxed cloth over leather breeches

▲ **SOURCE 3** *Three scenes from a leaflet about the Plague, published in 1666*

▼ **SOURCE 4** *In 1665 the Lord Mayor gave these orders to all Londoners to try to stop the Plague spreading*

- Examiners: to enquire what houses be visited [by illness] and what persons be sick, and of what diseases. And if they find any person sick of the infection the house shall be shut up for a month and none can leave the house. Every house infected to be marked with a red cross a foot long with these words: 'Lord Have Mercy Upon Us'.
- Searchers: women searchers to be appointed. They shall make a search and report whether the persons do die of the infection, or of what other diseases. No searcher be permitted to keep any shop or stall, or work as a laundress.
- Watchmen: for every infected house there be appointed watchmen, one for the day, and the other for the night. They have a special care that no person goes in or out of infected houses.
- Householders: every householder must keep the street before his door swept all the week long.
- Rakers and dog-killers: the filth of houses be daily carried away by the rakers. No hogs, cats or conies [rabbits] to be kept in the city. Dogs to be killed by the dog-killers.
- The burial of the dead must be always before sunrise or after sunset. No friend can accompany the corpse to church upon pain of having his house shut up. All the graves shall be at least six feet deep.

▼ ACTIVITY

1. Look at Source 2.
    a) What do you think 'plague water' might be?
    b) What measures did Samuel Pepys take to avoid catching the Plague?
    c) What measures did he see or hear of other people taking?
2. On your own copy of Source 3 write notes around the outside of each picture explaining in detail what is going on in that picture. You will need to refer to the rest of the evidence on pages 100 and 101 to help you.
3. Look at Source 4. Which of the jobs described do you think was the most dangerous?
4. Work in pairs. One of you is A, the other B.

    A Use Sources 1–4 to make a list of the methods people used to avoid the Plague in the seventeenth century. Then design a poster to be put up in London in 1665 telling people how to avoid the Plague. Include all the methods in your list.

    B Your teacher will tell you what actually caused the Plague. Use this information to design a poster telling people how to avoid the Plague.

    Discuss the differences between the two posters.

HOW DID LONDON CHANGE?

The Great Fire of London: 'a blessing in disguise'?

In September 1666 the Plague was still going strong. Then, early on the morning of Sunday 2 September, after a long hot summer, another disaster struck – the Great Fire of London.

London's buildings were made of wood and the houses were very close together, so fires could spread easily.

Fanned by an east wind, the fire was soon out of control. It spread quickly along the river-front. Buildings were blown up with gunpowder to stop the fire spreading, but it was too late. The fire was unstoppable.

▼ **SOURCE 5** *From the diary of Samuel Pepys*

Daytime, 2 September 1666 So I down to the waterside and there got a boat, and there saw a lamentable fire. Everybody endeavoured to remove their goods into the boats. Poor people staying in their houses almost till the fire touched them, and then running into boats or clamber from one pair of stairs by the waterside to another.

At last met my Lord Mayor in Canning Street – like a man exhausted . . . he cried like a fainting woman, 'Lord! What can I do? I am exhausted. People will not obey me. I have been pulling down houses, but the fire overtakes us faster than we can do . . .'.

So he left me and I walked home, seeing people almost distracted and no means to quench the fire. The houses were very thick thereabouts and full of burning matter such as pitch and tar in Thames Street, and warehouses of oil, wines and brandy.

Evening, 2 September Fire is still increasing and the wind great. All over the Thames, with one's face in the wind, you were almost burnt with a shower of fire-drops. This is very true – the houses were burnt by these drops and flakes of fire . . . five or six houses one from the other.

▼ **SOURCE 6** *A painting of the Great Fire, made not long after the event*

By Tuesday 4 September it looked as if the whole city would be lost. But then the wind dropped. The firefighters could begin to douse the flames. By Friday it was all over. The damage was assessed.

- 13,000 houses had been destroyed.
- 87 children were dead.
- 52 company halls (the backbone of London's trade and industry) had been destroyed.
- The total loss was £10 million, at a time when London's annual income was only £12,000.

> ▼ **SOURCE 7** *From the diary of John Evelyn*
>
> **7 September 1666**   I went this morning on foot from Whitehall to London Bridge and out to Moorfields, clambering over heaps of smouldering rubbish. The ground under my feet was so hot that it even burnt the soles of my shoes . . . I was not able to pass through any of the narrower streets, but kept to the widest. The ground and air, smoke and fiery vapour continued so intense that my hair was almost singed . . .
>
> Then I went towards Islington and Highgate, where one might have seen 200,000 people of all ranks and degrees lying by heaps of what they could save from the fire.

London rebuilt

There were many ambitious plans for rebuilding London. But none of them were adopted. There wasn't enough money to pay for such enormous changes and they would have taken too long. So it was decided to rebuild on the old street plan. Despite this quite a lot was achieved.

- Over 100 streets were widened.
- Timber was banned as a building material and red brick and white stone were used instead.
- The dirty, polluted Fleet River was canalised (straightened) and eventually covered over.
- 51 new churches were built, including a new St Paul's Cathedral. They were all designed by Sir Christopher Wren.
- By 1671, 9000 houses had been completed.

By the early eighteenth century, London was a cleaner and safer city. The streets and buildings looked as if they had been planned properly. For the first time rows of houses were built in the same style and the same size. London now had some of the most elegant buildings in Europe. The rebuilding also made it more difficult for the Plague to spread. After 1666 London never suffered another Plague epidemic.

▼ ACTIVITY

1. Much of London has been destroyed. Before the Great Fire London was dirty, unhealthy and overcrowded. Now there is an opportunity to rebuild. You have been asked to develop some plans for the rebuilding.
   a) What materials would you use for the new buildings: wood, brick or stone?
   b) Would you make the roads: narrow, wide, straight or winding?
   c) Would you lay out the streets on a grid pattern or put in crescents and other shapes?
   Ask your teacher for a copy of an outline map. Draw in your new road system and any other features you would like to see.

▼ DISCUSS

2. Which do you find most useful for telling you about the fire: the painting (Source 6) or the diary extracts (Sources 5 and 7)? Give reasons.
3. What do the diary extracts tell us about:
   a) why the fire spread so quickly along the river-front
   b) how the fire jumped between houses
   c) what was done to try to stop the fire
   d) the reactions of people to the fire?

HOW DID LONDON CHANGE?

London in the 1700s
In eighteenth-century London, life was changing.

Business
In the 1700s business and trade were growing in many parts of Britain. London was the financial powerhouse of this expansion. Banking and business grew quickly, with new offices being built all the time.

Trade
London was also Britain's biggest and busiest port. It became the centre of a rapidly expanding world trade. This trade brought products and foods to Britain that would have been completely unheard of 250 years earlier.

▼ **SOURCE 8** *From the journal of a seventeenth-century visitor to London*

Supper being finished they set on the table half a dozen pipes and a packet of tobacco.
   Smoking is the general custom for both women and men. They say it destroys the humours of the brain.

▲ **SOURCE 10** *The coat of arms of John Hawkins, a slave trader*

▼ **SOURCE 11** *From a London newspaper, 1744*

To be sold: a pretty little negro boy, about nine years old, and well limbed. He is to be seen at the Dolphin Tavern.

▼ **SOURCE 9** *An engraving of London in 1723*

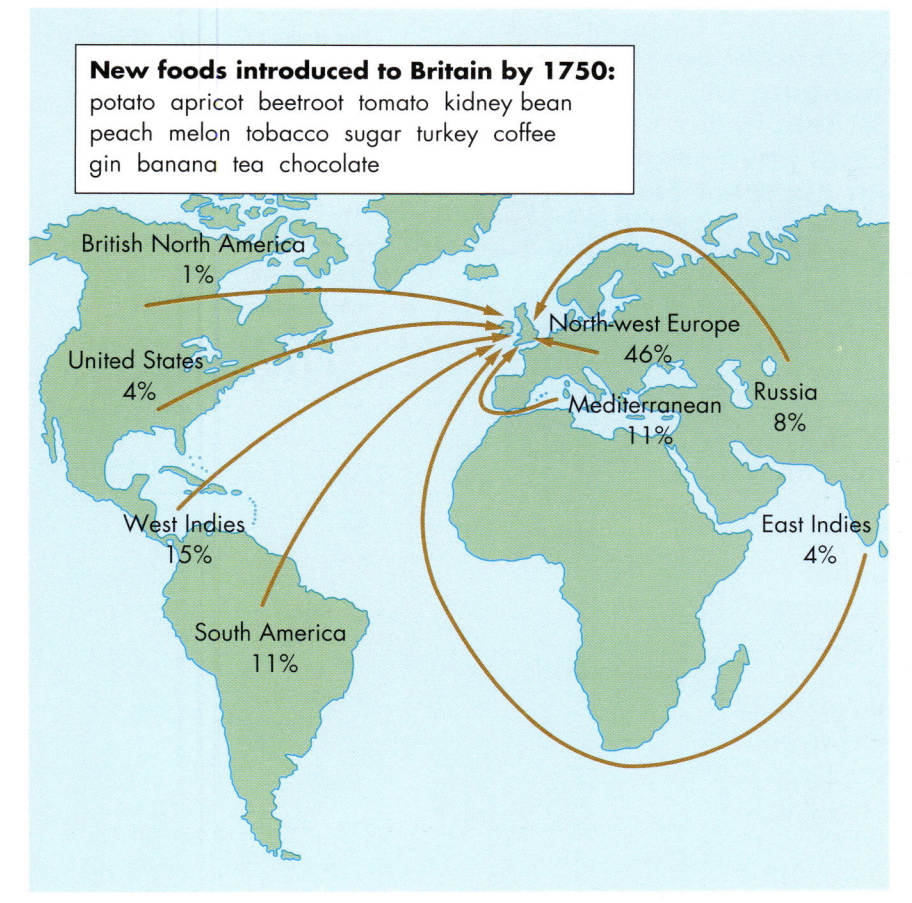

New foods introduced to Britain by 1750:
potato apricot beetroot tomato kidney bean peach melon tobacco sugar turkey coffee gin banana tea chocolate

British North America 1%
United States 4%
North-west Europe 46%
Mediterranean 11%
Russia 8%
West Indies 15%
East Indies 4%
South America 11%

▲ **SOURCE 12** *London's trade in 1750. The arrows show where London's main imports came from*

▲ **SOURCE 13** *A coffee house*

Slaves

London also became a centre for the infamous and cruel slave trade. Slave traders, such as John Hawkins (see Source 10), got rich by capturing people from West Africa and selling them as slaves to farmers in the Caribbean and North America.

From the 1570s onwards African people were also brought as slaves to Britain – mostly to London. Slave sales, such as the one referred to in Source 11, were held in pubs in London.

Most black people in England lived in London, but by no means all were slaves. Some had a trade. Some were entertainers and others were soldiers.

Newspapers

In 1702 Fleet Street became the centre of a flourishing new industry – newspaper publishing.

Coffee houses

Now people had time to relax and money to spend, coffee houses appeared where men would sit for hours reading the papers and discussing the latest political developments.

▼ ACTIVITY

You are a German visitor to London in 1750. Design a 'wish you were here' postcard to send home. On one side there should be a picture of some aspect of London. On the other side, describe some of the things you have seen in London.

A tour around Britain

▶▶ **In the previous enquiry you will have got an impression of London as a changing city. If you had travelled around the rest of Britain in the mid-1700s what kind of country would you have seen? Did one part of the country differ from another? Had things changed since 1500?**

In the 1720s the writer Daniel Defoe made several journeys round Britain and published his account of what he saw in a collection of letters called *A Tour Through the Whole Island of Great Britain*. You are going to follow him on his journeys.

All the written sources on pages 107–111 come from his book. All the pictures are from the eighteenth century and show the things that Defoe wrote about and would have seen.

Defoe travelled by all the means of transport available – by horse, foot, river barge and, most often, stage coach. By 1750 stage coaches were making regular runs between London and the main towns in Britain. In 1750 it took two and a half days to get to Birmingham and six days to get to Exeter. Horses were changed at an inn at the end of every 15 km 'stage'.

▶ **SOURCE 1** *The places mentioned in this enquiry*

▼ **SOURCE 2** *An engraving of Norwich, 1724. Norwich was the second largest city in England at this time*

The United Kingdom of Great Britain and Ireland

The United Kingdom included England, Wales, Scotland (together called Great Britain) and Ireland. In 1500 these were separate countries, each ruled in a different way. By the 1700s, they were all under the control of Parliament in London and had become the United Kingdom – a title we still use today. How did this happen? If you want to know, ask your teacher for your 'Making of the UK' worksheet.

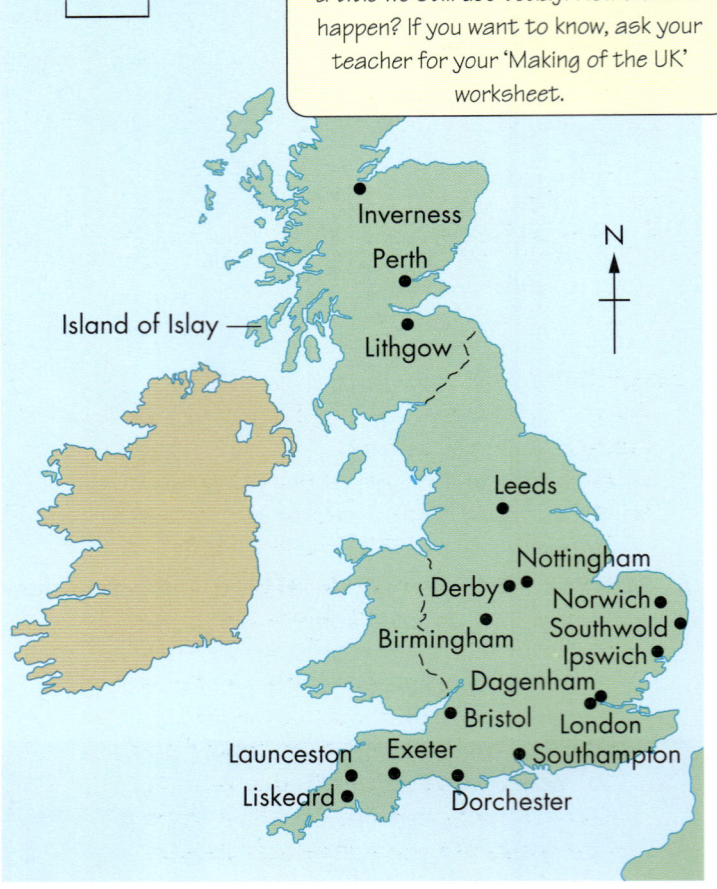

East Anglia

▼ **SOURCE 3** *The coastal area of Dagenham*

These lowlands are held by farmers, cow-keepers and grazing butchers who live in or near London. They buy large fat sheep in Smithfield market in September and keep them here till Christmas, when they sell them at a good price.

▼ **SOURCE 4** *Suffolk*

Here [Southwold] cattle are fattened with turnips. Suffolk is also famous for furnishing London with turkeys. More are bred here than in the rest of England. The geese and turkeys travel to London on foot.

▼ **SOURCE 5** *Norfolk*

When we come into Norfolk we see vast manufacture carried on by the Norwich weavers, who employ all the country round in spinning yarn for them. In and around Norwich 120,000 people are employed in woollen and silk manufacture.

▼ **SOURCE 6** *The land around Ipswich*

The country here is used chiefly for growing corn, most of which is shipped off for London. Sometimes they load corn here for Holland.

1 What different activities are mentioned in Sources 3–6?

2 What evidence is there that this part of the country was important for supplying London?

▼ **ACTIVITY**

Stage one: research
1. As you read pages 106–111 you will carry out some research.
   a) Make your own large copy of Source 1.
   b) Now, using a separate research sheet for each part of the country, make notes about the activities/jobs mentioned by Defoe. Note the trade routes that Defoe mentions.
   c) As you read you will come across star questions about the places Defoe visited. Unless specifically asked to do so, don't write separate answers to them. Simply use the question to help you complete your research sheets.

Stage two: paste up
2. Make a large display with your map at the centre and your research sheets around the outside. Use leader lines to link the sheets to the places.

Stage three: analysis
3. It is now time to analyse your findings. Look back at page 6. Do you think Defoe's Britain sounds more modern than Britain in 1500, or much the same? Are there any aspects of life seen by Defoe that you think had not changed much since 1500? Are there any which had changed a great deal?
4. Was Britain a modern country in the 1720s? Write two paragraphs to explain your answer using evidence from your research.

▼ **EXTRA**

5. It is 1750. Where in Britain would you least like to live? Where would you most like to live? Design an advertisement attracting people to move to where you would most like to live.

A TOUR AROUND BRITAIN

The West and Wales

> **SOURCE 7** *Dorchester*
>
> The Downs around Dorchester are exceedingly pleasant. There are 600,000 sheep fed on the Downs within six miles of the town. Farmers come to Burford Fair to buy them and take them back to Kent, Surrey and Oxfordshire.

People came from all over central and southern England to Wey Hill Fair. Design a poster advertising the fair. Tell people about all the things they can buy there.

▲ **SOURCE 8** *A drawing of Dorchester in 1750*

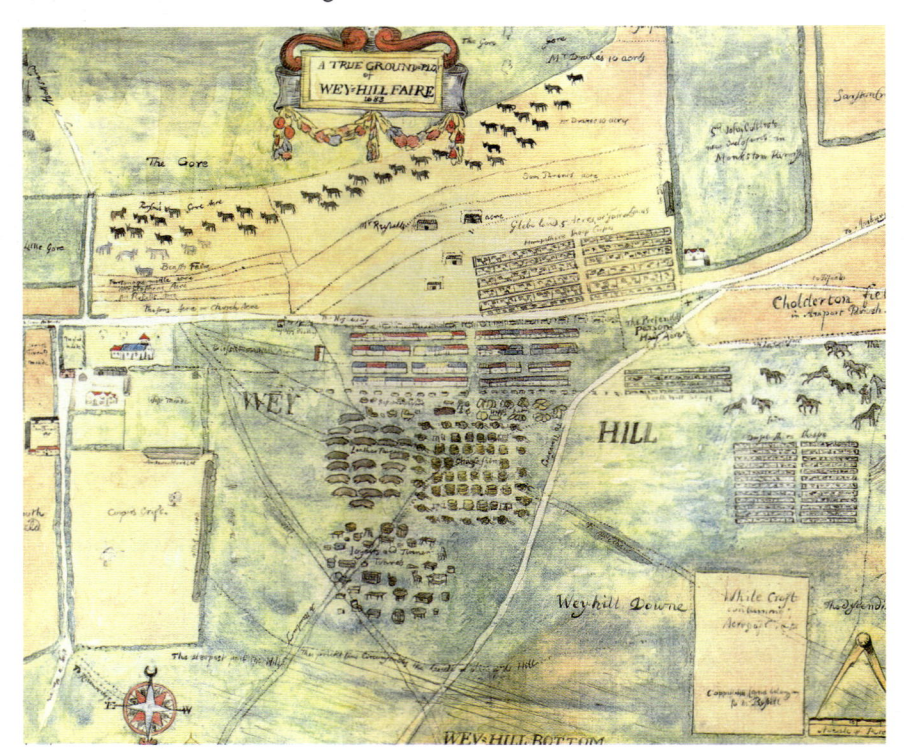

When Defoe visited Wey Hill Fair in the 1720s it was 'the greatest sheep fair this nation can show'.

As Defoe travelled into Cornwall, between Launceston and Liskeard, he found many tin mines with 'some of the richest veins of metal in the whole country'. These mines were hundreds of metres deep. They were drained by a new invention – the steam pump.

▲ **SOURCE 9** *A plan of Wey Hill Fair drawn in 1683*

◀ **SOURCE 10** *Bristol painted in the 1720s*

What activities can you see going on in this painting?

▼ **SOURCE 12** *A Cornish tin mine drawn in the 1770s*

What industries can you see going on?

▲ **SOURCE 11**
The different industries to be found on the Welsh coast in 1748

▼ **SOURCE 13** *Bristol was growing particularly rich from the slave trade*

The merchants of this city have the greatest trade other than London. The shopkeepers maintain carriers with all the main towns from Southampton to Nottingham.

A TOUR AROUND BRITAIN

The North

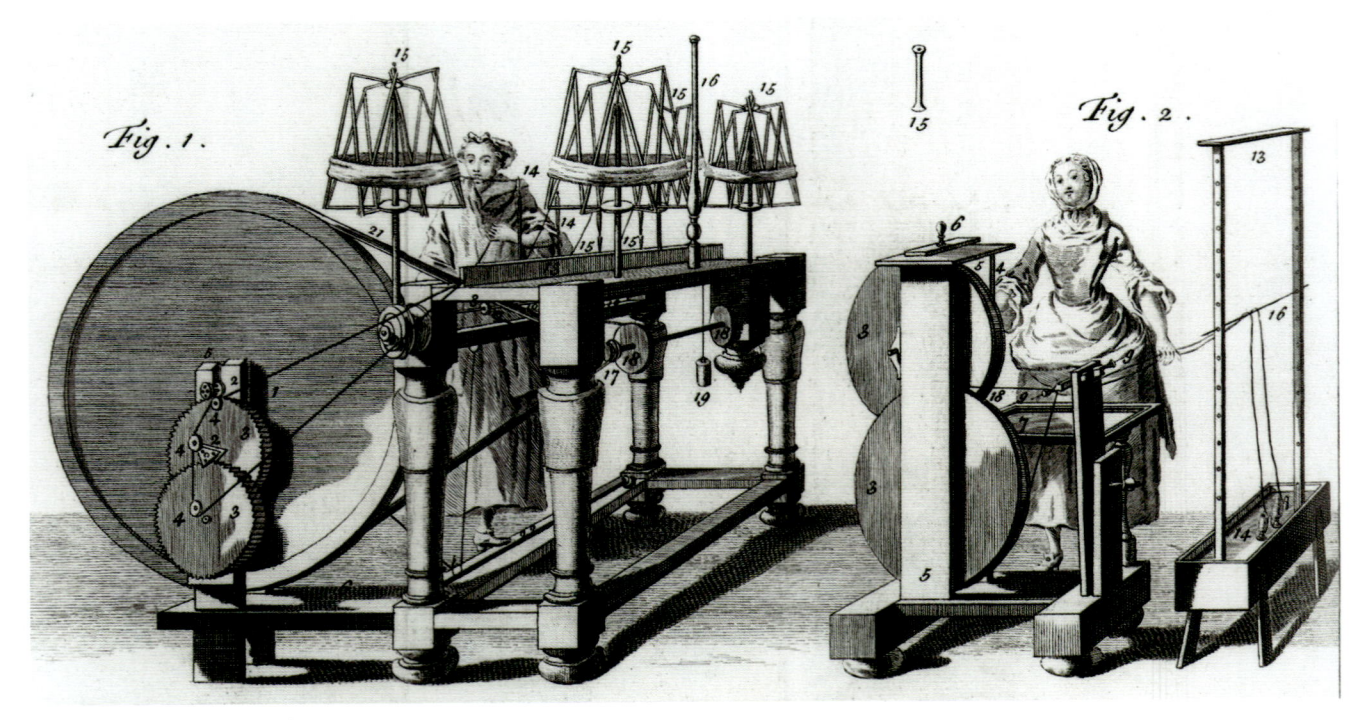

▲ **SOURCE 14** *The factory's machines for winding and twisting silk, drawn in 1747*

In Derby, Defoe saw 'the only silk mill in the country. It is turned by water and performs the labour of many hands.' Historians now believe that this was probably the first factory in England.

▼ **SOURCE 15** *Leeds cloth market took place in the main street twice a week*

You see ten and twenty thousand pounds of cloth, sometimes more, bought and sold in little more than an hour . . . for use at home . . . to send to London . . . or for overseas buyers from Holland and Germany.

▼ **SOURCE 16** *Derbyshire's lead miners*

The man was clothed all in leather. He had a leather cap without brims. We could not understand anything the man said. He was as pale as a dead corpse. Besides his basket of tools, he brought up with him [about 38 kg] of ore. This made him come heaving and struggling up. He was working at 60 fathoms [120m] deep. His wife and five children lived in a cave in the mountain. She washed the ore for 3d a day. But everything was clean and tidy and there was a side of bacon hanging. The children looked plump and fat and clean. Before we left we made up a little lump of money. As I pressed it into the woman's hand she dissolved into tears. She told me she had not seen so much money for many months.

Who do you think was poorer? The family in Source 16 or the family in Source 20?

Scotland

▼ **SOURCE 17** *Perth*

The chief business of the town is linen manufacture. The River Tay is navigable up to the town and they ship off a great quantity of linen, all for England.

▼ **SOURCE 18** *Lithgow*

The water of the loch here is said to be the best in Scotland for whitening the linen cloth. So a great deal of linen made in other parts of the country is brought here to be whitened.

◄ **SOURCE 19**
Wives carry their husbands out to their fishing boats at Inverness, 1725

> Write a detailed description of the house in Source 20. Include information about the number of children and animals living there, what people are doing, and how it is furnished.

▲ **SOURCE 20** *A house on the island of Islay, 1772*

Review 1500–1750: 'A picture of the period'

▼ REVIEW ACTIVITY

Here are six jigsaw pieces with segments of pictures which have appeared in this book.

1. Flip through the book and see if you can match each jigsaw piece with the picture it comes from.
2. Write a sentence for each piece, explaining what the picture it comes from shows.
3. Work with a partner. Together, choose one picture and prepare a speech about why it should be considered 'the picture of the period'. You should explain why the event which the picture illustrates was significant.
4. You might think a picture not here is more significant than the ones we've chosen. If so, explain your choice.
5. Hold a class debate and then a vote on which three pictures should be chosen to represent the period 1500–1750. The three you keep must summarise what you think the most important historical events or changes of the period were.

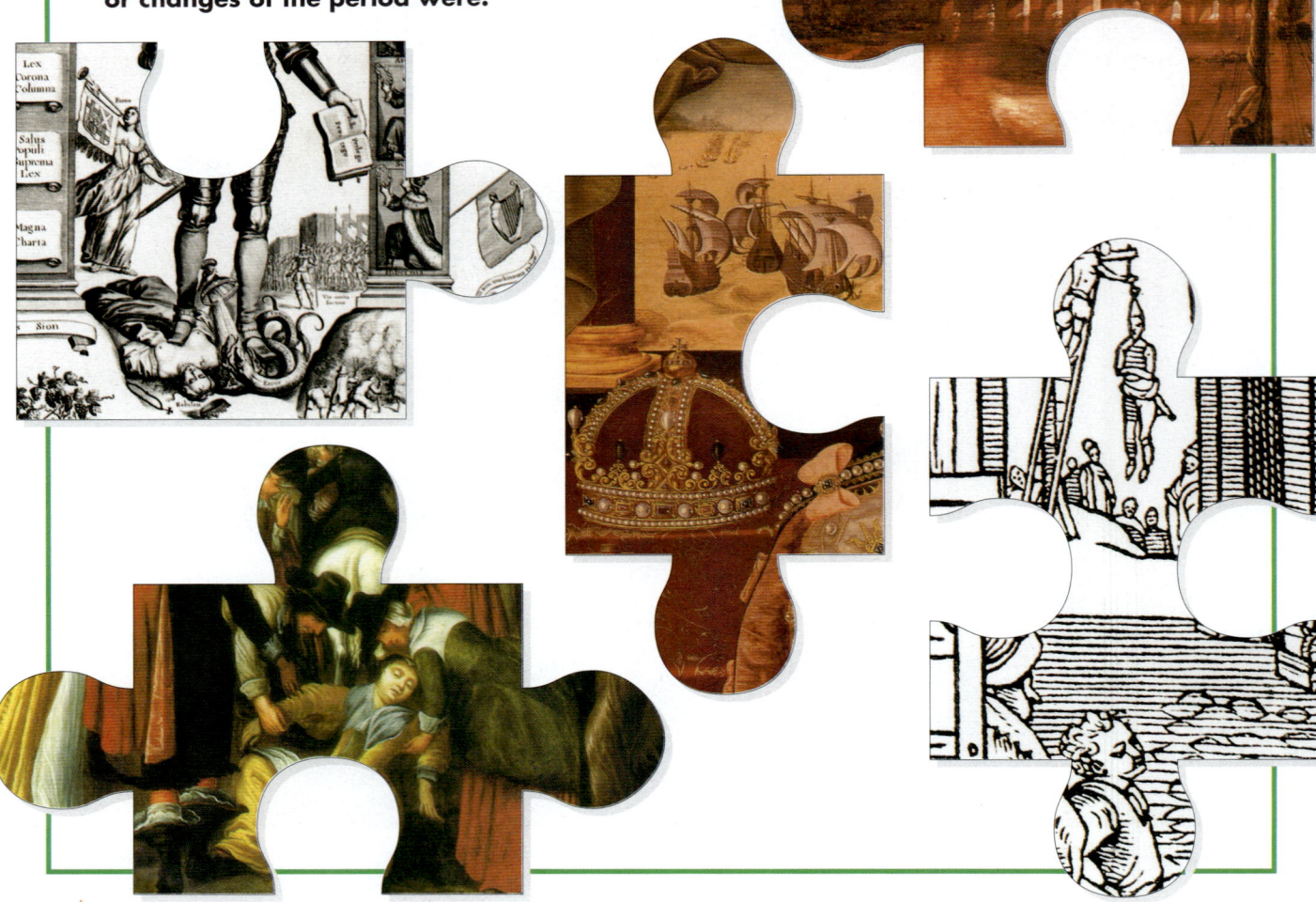

Glossary

CLERGY   all the people – such as priests, vicars, monks and nuns – who have been trained to perform religious duties in the Christian Church

EXTREMISTS   a person who holds extreme political or religious views

INFER   come to a conclusion based on facts and reasoning

INVENTORY   a complete list of someone's belongings, including their house and its contents, made when they died so that their property could be shared out fairly between relatives

JUSTICE OF THE PEACE (JP)   an official appointed by the government to keep law and order and try minor court cases in a town or county

MASS   a service in a Roman Catholic church, in memory of the Last Supper, when the body and blood of Christ, in the form of bread and wine, are consumed

OBITUARY   an account of the life of someone who has died

PARISH   the main division of local government until the nineteenth century. It was an area, usually an entire village, served by a single church

VAGRANT   a person who wanders about without a proper home or settled work

VESTMENTS   the official robes worn by the CLERGY during services

WET NURSE   a woman employed to breastfeed someone else's baby

Index

Armada 50–1
army 69, 88, 89

Babington, Anthony 49
beggars *see* vagrants

Catholicism and Catholics 32, 35
    Edward VI and 40–1
    Elizabeth I and 46–7, 49
    James I and 56–7, 59
    James II and 92, 93
    Mary I and 42–3
Cavaliers *see* Royalists
Cecil, Robert 57, 58, 59
Charles I 72, 73
    and Parliament 62–4, 66–73
    and religion 64, 65, 66, 67, 68
    and Scotland 64, 80
    trial and execution 80–3
Charles II 89, 92
childbirth and childcare 28–9
Civil War
    events leading up to 63–9
    life during 72–9
    timeline 62–3
cloth industry 6, 97, 107, 110, 111
Coram, Thomas 29
Cromwell, Oliver 73, 88–90

Defoe, Daniel 106–11
Diggers 84

Edward VI 40–1
Elizabeth I 44–7, 50–5
Evelyn, John 103

family life 24–9
farming 6, 13, 107, 108
Fawkes, Guy 56, 57, 58
Fifth Monarchists 85

gentry 7, 16–19, 72, 89
Grand Remonstrance 68
Great Fire of London 102–3
Gunpowder Plot 56–9

Harley, Lady Brilliana 76–7
Henry VIII 34–9
houses 16–23
    gentry 16–19
    middle classes 20–1

James I 56–7, 59, 98
James II 92–3

Laud, Archbishop 64, 65, 67
legal system 66, 67, 85, 92, 98
Levellers 85
London 100–3
    changes in 103–5

marriage 26–7
    Elizabeth I and 44–5
Mary I 42–3
Mary, Queen of Scots 48–9
medicine 96, 97
mining 6, 97, 108, 109, 110
monasteries, dissolution of 13, 36–9

New Model Army 73, 85, 88
Nineteen Propositions 69

Parliament 88
    Charles I and 63–4, 66–9, 72, 80–3
Parliamentarians (Roundheads) 72, 73
Pepys, Samuel 27, 100, 102
Philip II of Spain 43, 50
Plague 100–1, 103
Poor Law 14
poor people 10–15, 26
portraits 24–5, 51–3
printing industry 84, 97, 99, 101, 105
Protestantism and Protestants 33
    Charles I and 68
    Edward VI and 40–1
    Elizabeth I and 46–7
    Henry VIII and 35
    Mary I and 42–3
Puritans 64, 65, 76–7, 86–7

religion
    Charles I and 64, 65, 66, 67, 68
    Edward VI and 40–1
    Elizabeth I and 46–7, 49
    Henry VIII and 34–9
    James I and 56–7
    Mary I and 42–3
rich people 16–19, 24–5, 26, 29
Roundheads *see* Parliamentarians
Royalists (Cavaliers) 72, 73

science 96–7
Scotland 48, 64, 80, 111
Ship Money 64, 67
slavery 104, 105, 109
social groups 7

taxation 14, 63, 64, 66, 67
Tour Through the Whole Island of Great Britain, A see Defoe
trade 104, 105, 109, 110

vagrants (beggars) 10–11, 14

wet nurses 28, 29
William and Mary of Orange 93, 94
Winter, Thomas 58
witchcraft 98–9

Acknowledgements

Photographs reproduced by kind permission of:

Cover Scottish National Portrait Gallery/By permission of the Earl of Rosebery; **p.iii** *t* 'A Fete at Bermondsey', Hatfield House/Fotomas UK (detail), *c* Hulton Getty (detail), *b* National Gallery, London, UK/Bridgeman Art Library (detail); **p.iv** *l* Woburn Abbey, Bedfordshire, UK/Bridgeman Art Library (detail), *r* Private Collection/Bridgeman Art Library (detail); **p.1** *l* Mary Evans Picture Library (detail), *c* Hulton Getty (detail); **p.4** *clockwise* Katz Pictures (detail), Bodleian Library/University of Oxford (RSL.CR.N.85) (detail), Fotomas Index UK, Bridgeman Art Library (detail), Reproduced by courtesy of the British Museum (detail), Fortean Picture Library (detail), Scottish National Portrait Gallery/By permission of the Earl of Rosebery (detail), Bridgeman Art Library (detail); **p.5** 'A Fete at Bermondsey', Hatfield House/Fotomas UK; **p.8** *t* Kunsthistorisches Museum, Vienna/ Bridgeman Art Library, *l* MS 311 Virgil/ Reproduced courtesy of Earl of Leicester, Holkham Hall, *r* Katz Pictures; **p.9** *l* Victoria and Albert Museum/Bridgeman Art Library, *r* Katz Pictures; **p.11** *l* Katz Pictures, *c* Private Collection/ Bridgeman Art Library, *b* Katz Pictures; **p.15** Private Collection/Bridgeman Art Library; **p.16** *t* Photo by A.F. Kersting, *b* National Trust Photographic Library/Mike Williams; **p.17** *t* AA Photo Library, *cl & cr* Old House, Hereford, Courtesy of Herefordshire Council, *b* National Trust Photographic Library; **p.21** *tr* Photo by A.F. Kersting, *tl* and *b* Reproduced by permission of Plymouth City Museums and Art Gallery; **p.22** *t* Museum of London Picture Library, *c* The Art Archive/London Museum/Eileen Tweedy, *b* Trustees of the Victoria and Albert Museum; **p.23** *tl* The Art Archive/ Staffordshire University School of Art, *tr* Museum of London Picture Library, *cr* The Art Archive/ Staffordshire University School of Art, *br* The Art Archive/ London Museum/Eileen Tweedy, *bc, bl & cl* Museum of London Picture Library; **p.25** *t* Reproduced by permission of the Marquess of Bath, Longleat House, Warminster, Wiltshire, *b* Yale Centre for British Art, Paul Mellon Collection, USA/Bridgeman Art Library; **p.26** Mary Evans Picture Library; **p.28** Mary Evans Picture Library; **p.29** Bodleian Library/University of Oxford (RSL.CR.N.85); **p.35** *b* Fotomas Index UK; **p.43** Private Collection/Bridgeman Art Library; **p.50** both Woburn Abbey, Bedfordshire, UK/ Bridgeman Art Library (detail); **p.51** Woburn Abbey, Bedfordshire, UK/Bridgeman Art Library; **p.52** *t* Private Collection/Ken Welsh/Bridgeman Art Library, *bl* Philip Mould Historical Portraits Ltd, London, UK/Bridgeman Art Library, *br* The Royal Collection © 2000, Her Majesty Queen Elizabeth II; **p.53** *t* Corsham Court Collection, *c* Courtesy of the Trustees of the Victoria and Albert Museum, *b* By courtesy of The National Portrait Gallery, London; **p.57** Private Collection/Bridgeman Art Library; **p.58** Fotomas Index UK; **p.59** Private Collection/ Bridgeman Art Library; **p.61** Hulton Getty; **p.65** *t* Fotomas Index UK, *b* Hulton Getty, **p.73** *both* The Ancient Art and Architecture Collection Ltd; **p.74** *t & c* Mary Evans Picture Library, *b* Private Collection/Bridgeman Art Library; **p.75** Fotomas Index UK; **p.78–9** Walker Art Gallery, Liverpool, UK/Bridgeman Art Library Board of Trustees: National Museums and Galleries on Merseyside; **p.80** Private Collection/Bridgeman Art Library; **p.82** Ashmolean Museum, Oxford; **p.83** Scottish National Portrait Gallery/By permission of the Earl of Rosebery; **p.84** Fotomas Index UK; **p.86** Fotomas Index UK; **p.90** *t* Fotomas Index UK, *b* Private Collection/Bridgeman Art Library; **p.95** National Gallery, London, UK/ Bridgeman Art Library; **p.97** *t* Fotomas Index UK, *b* Ann Ronan Picture Library; **p.98** Private Collection/Bridgeman Art Library; **p.99** *tl & tr* Fortean Picture Library, *b* Hulton Getty; **p.101** Private Collection Bridgeman Art Library; **p.102** The Art Archive/ London Museum/Eileen Tweedy; **p.104** Reproduced by courtesy of the Trustees of the British Museum; **p.105** The Art Archive/ London Museum/Eileen Tweedy; **p.106–7** British Library ©; **p.108** *t* Bodleian Library, University of Oxford (W34884), *b* Courtesy of Andover Museum; **p.109** *t* Bristol City Museum and Art Gallery, UK/Bridgeman Art Library, *bl* Pembrokeshire Record Office, Dyfed/Paul Harrison, *br* Royal Institution of Cornwall, Royal Cornwall Museum, Truro ©; **p.110** Bodleian Library, University of Oxford (Per 2705e 552/1); **p.111** *both* Scottish Ethnological Archive, National Museums of Scotland ©; **p.112** *clockwise* Fotomas Index UK (detail), The Art Archive/London Museum/Eileen Tweedy (detail), Private Collection/Bridgeman Art Library (detail), Woburn Abbey, Bedfordshire, UK/ Bridgeman Art Library (detail), Scottish National Portrait Gallery/By permission of the Earl of Rosebery (detail), Fotomas Index UK (detail).

t = top, *b* = bottom, *c* = centre, *l* = left, *r* = right

Every effort has been made to contact copyright holders, but if any have been inadvertently overlooked the Publisher will be pleased to make the necessary arrangements at the earliest opportunity.